D0065323

DECADENCE AND OBJECTIVITY

Decadence and Objectivity

LAWRENCE HAWORTH

University of Toronto Press

Toronto and Buffalo

Toronto and Buffalo
Printed in Canada

Library of Congress Cataloging in Publication Data

Haworth, Lawrence.
Decadence and objectivity.

Includes index.
1. Social values. 2. Social ethics. I. Title.
HM111.H28 301.5 77-4972
ISBN 0-8020-5387-4

This book has been published during the
Sesquicentennial year of the University of Toronto

FOR ALISON

Say you have a son and daughter, and in a private moment ask:
'How would you have things work out for them?'
'So they find a talent, a niche in which to practise it, do it well, and know that. Also, so they are at ease.'
'What do you most regret?'
'That they haven't found a world – that I haven't had a world to give them – in which these results are striven for, but that they opened their eyes on something rather different.'
'And do you despair then?'
'No, because they (and their friends) are resourceful.'

Contents

Perhaps it is this specter that most haunts working men and women: the planned obsolescence of people that is of a piece with the planned obsolescence of the things they make. Or sell. It is perhaps this fear of no longer being needed in a world of needless things that most clearly spells out the unnaturalness, the surreality of much that is called work today.

Fireman:

I worked in a bank. You know, it's just paper. It's not real. Nine to five and it's shit. You're lookin' at numbers. But I can look back and say, 'I helped put out a fire. I helped save somebody.' It shows something I did on this earth.

Carpenter/Poet:

All of a sudden something falls into place. Suppose you're driving an eight-penny galvanized finishing nail into this siding. Your whole universe is rolled onto the head of that nail. Each lick is sufficient to justify your life. You say, 'Okay, I'm not trying to get this nail out of the way so I can get onto something more important. There's nothing more important. It's right there.' And it goes – pow!

Studs Terkel, *Working*

Preface

Many people feel something is seriously wrong with modern life and institutions and want to see basic changes. We need, they say, a new philosophy. But what they think *is* wrong varies widely, and for the most part the specific changes sought are only alluded to vaguely. The call for a new philosophy is seldom answered, almost never with the *seriousness* that attends diagnosis of the problems.

In the following pages I try to shift the emphasis. I begin, in Chapters 2 to 4, with a brief discussion of some problems everyone agrees are central. But I assume that these are well understood. No one needs to be reminded of their dimensions or seriousness. This allows taking as my effective point of departure the conflict between two standard responses to the problems: individualism and collectivism. One may think of New York City and a Chinese commune – not as we find them but as we would were their blemishes removed: New York without its racial problems and wide discrepancies between rich and poor, a city of leisure where the individual freedoms and affluence of some don't rest on the restriction and poverty of others; the commune freed from the dead hand of the Party, an autonomous group who collectively and openly fix their own goals and whose members find *their* well-being in a life that contributes as well to the well-being of the entire group.

These idealizations of New York City and the Chinese commune form two models of a better setting for human life. They express two sharply contrasting views of how to refocus life so that deficiencies in present practices are overcome. Each model points to a new lifestyle and a new set of values. One focuses on leisure, the other on work. When the models are sympathetically described, many find themselves equally attracted to both. This is unfortunate, since their opposition is such that having either setting – New York or the commune – involves to that extent not having the other. They emphatically don't go together.

This conflict is analysed from various points of view, in Chapters 5 and 6, with an eye to reaching a constructive resolution. It would obviously be of some interest to discover a set of values and a lifestyle that incorporate the positive features of both the commune ideal and that of a city of leisure. And if in addition we could identify some of the major changes in established practices that would complement such a change in values and lifestyle, the basis would be laid for a new philosophy appropriate to our own times and circumstances, and sensitive to our own twenty-first century problems.

In pursuing this rather ambitious goal I am led by consideration of the issues to a point of view to which, with some hesitation, I give the name 'objectivity' – I say with hesitation because the term has connotations such as coldness and lack of concern that I don't intend, and has been associated with repugnant features of modern life, such as bureaucracy and narrow pursuit of economic efficiency, that I have no wish to defend. Here, instead, objectivity is used as an approximate synonym for impartiality or fairness, understood as a personal outlook or stance, with the added connotation of one's being oriented outwards, on *objects*, and of locating the significance of one's life in those objects rather than in their impact on oneself or on the groups with which one identifies. From the perspective that the ideal of objectivity affords, present modes of life that are most dangerous to us are signs of 'decadence.' Hence my title.

Objectivity, considered as the dominant theme of a lifestyle, may appear in different guises, depending on the type of activity being carried on. In our relationships with the natural world, to be objective is to be 'responsible.' By means of this notion I attempt, in Chapter 2, to stake out a middle ground between two extremes – that of single-mindedly rejecting all interference by man with nature and that of sanctioning any such interference that can be defended as serving the distinctive interests of mankind.

'Responsibility' refers to the attitude that the non-human realm is not there simply to serve man, that it is not merely a domain of 'things' wholly meant to be used, but that neither is it appropriate to adopt a custodial role in terms of which nature is treated as a 'preserve.' Roughly, the ground staked out between these extremes is that on which a person, being responsible in his dealings with the non-human realm, brings to bear his own distinctively human competence, creativity, but expresses this not by exploiting nature for the satisfaction of human needs but rather by building a world that is true to the constraints and possibilities of the material he is working with.

In work, the carrying on of an occupation, objectivity shows itself as 'professionalism,' an idea first suggested by noticing, in Chapter 3, the way in which a collegial community of professionals provides in a twentieth-century setting the values experienced by less technologically advanced people in spatially defined village communities and neighbourhoods. The ideal of professionalism, as a way of catching up the aspirations of conscientious people who possess a distinctive competence and who instinctively define themselves by reference to the occupation in which this competence is expressed, is pervasive – despite the fact that our philosophers, moralists, and social critics have scarcely even noted the existence of the ideal, much less contributed to its clarification and assessment. As the argument of the book proceeds, principally because of the importance I am led to attach to the idea of a life work, professionalism becomes increasingly central to the entire discussion. Following an account of the meaning of professionalism in Chapter 8, largely carried out by contrasting this with communism, I consider in Chapter 9 some of the changes in work and in the principles for distribution of income that are involved in the idea of professionalizing a society's economy.

My third leading idea is 'leisureliness,' introduced in Chapter 4 in the course of considering the contrast between work and leisure as these are currently carried on. But the logic of the argument by which the conception of work is replaced by that of professionalism suggests a comparable redefinition of leisure from the sense of 'free time' or 'discretionary time' to that of unrushed activity in which what one is doing and undergoing is savoured and enjoyed for its own sake rather than sacrificed to some imagined future benefits. Leisureliness in this sense is a distinctive mode of objectivity, and thus complements professionalism and responsibility. Finally, in Chapter 10, I consider some of the social changes that would enhance leisureliness in modern life, principally by describing neighbourhood as the natural habitat for leisure.

My idea is that these three notions – responsibility, professionalism, and leisureliness – form the focal points in one coherent but realistic conception of a distinctively contemporary lifestyle. In sketching out this conception I have primarily attempted to bring the whole picture into view, and this within the space of a fairly short book. Thus, I have deliberately stopped short of detailed elaboration of particular aspects of the conception – out of a fear that if the reader is invited to look too closely at too many of the trees he will lose his feel for the size and shape of the forest. In particular, the reader with a practical bent, who wonders what we must *do* to realize the ideals described here will receive little guidance. I wish it were otherwise. I am far from believing that merely coming to hold the ideals is sufficient; but it is at least necessary. The book, then, is a start, but much remains to be done.

Its publication has been made possible by grants from the Social Science Research Council of Canada, using funds provided by the Canada Council, and from the Publications Fund of the University of Toronto Press.

DECADENCE AND OBJECTIVITY

CHAPTER ONE

Decadence

A decadent person is one who lacks an animating vision of an ideal state of affairs. The idea of being motivated by a desire to contribute to the perfection of the whole is foreign to him. Or distasteful. He has ideals, perhaps. He may pursue something for himself – comfort, power, acclaim, health – or be absorbed in a private sphere, most often his family, and devote himself to its well-being. But in these concerns he shuts out the world; they fix for him the boundaries of the territory that really matters – beyond lie only threats or the utilities with which he decorates his private spheres.

In this sense most people are decadent: they live largely in private spheres and value the public domain for the contribution it makes toward enhancing their private lives. Their decadence reflects a comparable condition of the social system. In large part our lives are decadent not just in fact but in conception. This, a fairly recent development, is illustrated by changes in the two most compelling social ideals of our era, capitalism and democracy. Not long ago it was generally believed that capitalism and democracy had quite definite meanings and that they adequately described prevailing economic and political institutions. Moreover, most people, and not only the outstanding beneficiaries of the institutions, were committed to a set of values – including work, thrift, and profit – that they regarded as objectively good rather than mere means to their own welfare, and as sustained by and sustaining elements of the economic and political system. In consequence, capitalism and democracy seemed to have intrinsic worth. So far as the institutions formed a framework for people's lives with which they could relate everyday affairs, they enjoyed that tacit sense of larger meaning that is the hallmark of a non-decadent existence.

Today it is anachronistic to defend capitalism and democracy in the old way. The meanings of the terms are problematic, and it is an open question whether our economic and political institutions sufficiently satisfy any of the competing definitions to warrant their continued use. There is no longer a sense of the larger social significance of work, thrift, and profit. They are sometimes valued, but not for their role in a way of life. Instead, the benefit they bring to the individual who works, saves, and profits is emphasized. The shift has focused attention on the instrumental values of capitalism and democracy. They are not viewed as particularly admirable institutions in themselves but are accepted, so far as they are accepted, as reasonably adequate ways of bringing benefits to the private lives of citizens. Work, thrift, and profit, conceived in the old way as moral values, are replaced by gross national product. Capitalism is justified as an effective manner of organizing economic life so that we may be assured a high and increasing GNP. Except among fanatics, a high GNP is not valued for itself but for the number of jobs and the level of consumption it underwrites. And democracy is conceived not as an ideal form of political community that one might identify with as being itself admirable, but as an effective manner of resolving conflicts of interest among citizens, justified by its supposed capacity of assuring optimal satisfaction of people's wants.

These current conceptions of democracy and capitalism may of course be seen as illustrations of the popular idea that 'the state exists for the individual, not the individual for the state.' And so they are. That this aphorism is so widely and uncritically held testifies to the extent of our decadence. It also points up the danger of slipping without notice from a descriptive to an evaluative interpretation of the claim that our social system is largely decadent. For if descriptively to be decadent is to lack an animating vision of an ideal by which one is pointed beyond one's own personal concerns and private spheres, in its evaluative use it suggests rottenness and a stench of putrefaction, a certain way of being reprehensible. And the evaluation is not established by merely mentioning the features of our lives and of our conception of our institutions that support the claim that we are decadent in the descriptive sense.[1]

In later chapters I shall give reasons for thinking that the evaluation is apt – for thinking that, despite the appearance of self-evidence enjoyed by the claim that 'the state exists for the individual,' a society founded on this idea is wrongly oriented. Two distinct lines of argument may be pointed to. First, when a group of people orient their lives around private, self-referring concerns, the public sphere, which in any case supports their lifestyle, is in danger of neglect and deterioration. The sphere in which they have a common, co-operative life will be perceived as merely instrumental to their private concerns and they are likely to become actively involved in protecting it only in the face of transpar-

1 See especially M. Harrington, *The Accidental Century* (New York, 1966). Harrington uses the term 'decadence' in roughly the sense intended here and contrasts it with other, more familiar, uses (chap. 1).

ent threats to those concerns. Our present inability to detach ourselves from the goal of economic growth, despite widespread awareness of the public problems created by its pursuit, shows how real this danger is.

Second, one may also point to the self-defeating character of decadence, to the fact that, generally, it doesn't work, even in its own terms. The problem isn't created by people pursuing pleasure, but by the kind of objects in which their pleasure is sought. There is reason to think that the dissatisfaction with their lives that affluent people often experience is not a result of not being affluent enough but of their using their considerable resources to finance an essentially private lifestyle. Most people want and need to be *useful*, only often they find themselves in settings that don't elicit this in a comprehensive way. The resulting dissatisfaction may appear in different guises – as boredom or ennui, as more or less constant dis-ease and distraction, as a deep sense that one's life has no point and that one lacks *worth*.

Growing numbers of people are concerned about our decadence. Their concern is prompted by a variety of experiences and considerations. Some are moved by radical disillusion. Having experienced the meaninglessness of a society that, in its own terms, should be working very well for them, they have begun to grope for alternatives. One result is a new admiration for China, the best available example of a non-decadent society. Her citizens largely forswear personal ambitions and private interests, and gain their primary sense of the significance of their lives from the ways they contribute to 'building the new China.' Moreover, her institutions are directed toward consolidating this orientation. In one sense it works: large numbers of people find and seize an opportunity to make their contribution, and experience thereby both liberation and significance. So much must be insisted on, despite the necessity to add that China forms a closed society – her political system appears to be dictatorial and her citizens apparently find little encouragement of spontaneity and limited avenues for development and expression of individuality.

Others are moved by realization that although the pace of social change is phenomenal, it is largely without direction. We are careening into the future with little sense of where we are going or what our destination ought to be. In these circumstances, responsible people are mainly managers, caught up in day-to-day problems created by the blind journey. Preoccupied with dodging obstacles immediately ahead and with keeping us more or less upright, they have no time, energy, or capability for bringing overall coherence to the changes that wash over us.

Still others stress the self-destructiveness of the course we are on. A few elementary calculations, by which rates of growth of environmental demand are related with estimates of capability to respond to the demand, yield dates when, on various assumptions, we may expect the system under which we live to collapse. Optimistic assumptions push the date comfortably forward into the twenty-first century – our children may not experience it – while pessimistic assumptions move it back into our own lifetimes.[2]

That the social system is meaningless, directionless, and self-destructive – these are reflections that move people to the edge of decadence. By these different routes they arrive at a common need. To find meaning and direction, and to avoid self-destruction, a compelling image of the future is required, a model of the human world as it might be and as we would like it to be. The very circumstances that create the need, expand the scope of alternatives it is realistic to consider and make radical proposals feasible. Meaninglessness and directionlessness imply a vacuum within which there is readiness to consider any model, and the sense of imminent catastrophe creates an urgency that overrides hesitations stemming from desire to 'stick to the tried and true.' To meet the requirements the model may, indeed should, imply a radical departure.

II

Social reality is more complex than any model a person may use to talk about it, and this is especially true of the models in which one tries to bring together one's hopes for the future. The model is an idealization that catches up only some of the facts. In this respect it resembles a map which doesn't attempt to portray every feature of the terrain mapped but abstracts some and describes their interrelationships while ignoring everything else. Thus, the relative distances between places may be precisely replicated but not relative elevations. Similarly, a model of the future will pick out certain features as being peculiarly important and ignore the rest. Inevitably, then, it will simplify the reality it refers to.

The important feature of a model of the future is that it represents the characteristic practices of a society as having a point. Simplification and abstraction are unavoidable, since no account, however lengthy, of what people are or should be really getting at in a society is capable of including all the motives at work there. One must stress the major truths, and what we take these to be will depend very much on our purposes in stressing anything at all. It is not necessary for the model to simplify to the extent of mentioning just one point or outcome as forming the organizing principle, but it may be convenient to do so, particularly when the model refers to an idealized rather than an actual state of affairs.

The two interesting features of the point of a social system are that it deter-

2 See especially D. Meadows *et al.*, *The Limits to Growth* (New York, 1972).

mines the system's *focal value* and its *validating experiences*. A focal value provides the point of view from which it is possible to see a society as forming a system; then one may grasp the arrangement of its characteristic practices. When the manner in which these practices contribute to production of the focal value (or, so far as the society lacks coherence, the ways they tend to defeat it) is grasped, the important features of their relations with one another are disclosed. In the same way, making sense of a complex sequence of movements requires understanding the end they are directed toward, with reference to which the movements fall into place and are themselves understandable.

A focal value is not itself a purpose. It would, indeed, be an indefensible simplification to represent a society as having but one purpose. Instead, its focal value is a feature of all or most of its major purposes, the feature that accounts for their being pursued. Thus, many idealizations of Western society represent it as ordered by the focal value of consumption. Consuming is seen as the activity that members of the society regard as finally valuable, and the significance of the characteristic practices is associated with their manner of contributing to or detracting from consumption. Aristotle, by contrast, constructed a model in which the focal value was intellectual virtue, or, more narrowly, contemplation, a choice that relegates consumption to the status of a means to which no great importance is attached. When consumption is taken as the focal value, contemplation must be seen as either irrelevant or 'counterproductive.' The differences in social and physical design suggested by any consistent pursuit of these contrasting focal values are profound. A city that would be seen as well-ordered under the assumption that its focal value is contemplation would seem poorly designed when apprehended in terms of the focal value of consumption. It is evident that the first decision to be made in framing a model for the future concerns the focal value around which we wish our lives to be ordered.

Focal values are met by members of a society in validating experiences. When we accept a way of picturing our life with others, by seeing it as brought to a focus around some value, we are led to identify certain central activities the satisfying experience of which would validate the system in our eyes – if anything would. In a society that makes consumption a focal value, a prime validating experience will be that associated with activities around the Christmas tree the morning of December 25, when the presents are being opened and the air is redolent with scents of new commodities. In a society that makes contemplation a focal value, a prime validating experience will be the pleasures of leisurely philosophical dialogue. It is true that many people enjoy both opening Christmas presents and philosophizing, on some level of sophistication at least. But what is of interest is the order of priorities.

A pointed illustration is provided by Plato's dialogue, *The Symposium*, the setting of which is a banquet involving nearly a dozen people eating and drinking far into the night. The dialogue is largely taken up with speeches in praise of beauty and love by the symposiast-revellers. And yet nowhere is there specific reference to food or eating. To one whose tacit order of priorities ranks consumption above speculation, it is as if an accomplished playwright were to write a play in which all of the actors are members of a team, playing a game, but were to make no reference to the score, the outcome, even the action itself.

To the two-mentioned features of a social model, focal value and validating experience, a third should be added, idealized character type. If the members of a society conceive their life together so that they are able to identify certain central experiences as validating their characteristic practices, they are likely also to identify appropriate heroes, ideal character types who may or may not exist, who possess the traits and appurtenances that enable one to have and appreciate the validating experiences. In a consumption-oriented society, Hugh Heffner might qualify – equipment-strewn pad, jet airplane, playmates, successful money-maker. In Aristotle's model, the philosopher, Socrates in particular, is such a type – when convicted of corrupting the youth by discussing philosophy with them, he tells the court that a fitting sentence would be a pension from the city so that he might return to the agora and ply his trade.

Choice of the term 'consumer-oriented' to characterize Western society may be questioned from at least two points of view. It may be held that it is insensitive to the diversity of Western society and so oversimplifies a complex reality. And it may be held that, in light of this diversity, the appropriate description is not 'consumer-oriented' but 'libertarian.' The latter term refers to institutionalized tolerance of alternative lifestyles, a firm resolve to accommodate the widest possible variance in personal aspirations, style, and tastes, restricted only by the need to sustain them all in a viable scheme.[3]

I accept the first objection, amended to read 'simplifies' rather than 'oversimplifies.' Whether the simplification is excessive depends on whether it is responsible for distortion in the conclusions that follow. The reader must wait and judge for himself.

The second objection reaches farther, since it may prompt dissatisfaction with all talk about preferred focal values and lifestyles for a society as a whole. If we take our libertarianism seriously, must we not reject any attempt to identify a specific focal value or lifestyle as preferred for an entire society? For this is to attempt to decide for people something they must decide for themselves. And if a single focal value were accepted, would that not imply loss of the variety libertarians (properly) cherish?

3 In the recent literature the two most solid expressions of 'libertarianism' are those by Peter Strawson, 'Social Morality and Individual Ideal,' in *Philosophy*, XXXVI (1961), and Isaiah Berlin, 'Two Concepts of Liberty,' in *Four Essays on Liberty* (Oxford, 1969).

The second objection, then, has two forms. It questions the appropriateness of describing present society as consumer-oriented rather than libertarian. And it questions any conception of 'a better social order' that does not give due weight to the libertarian enthusiasm for variety. Fortunately, the key to replies to both forms is provided by the same observation: libertarianism, in the sense of tolerance of diversity, is not necessarily incompatible with a society's having adopted, for the most part, a single focal value - whether that be consumption or professionalism. Not *necessarily* incompatible: whether incompatible in fact depends on how the society mainly pursues the focal value in question. Thus, consumption is a highly abstract characterization of a society's focal value, compatible with great variation in specific lifestyles by which it is concretely pursued. And the society that does pursue it in manifold ways may both *prize* that variety and also tolerate those minorities whose lifestyles do not exemplify the focal value at all. Similarly, it is possible (and I hope to have achieved this in the following pages) to define a preferred focal value that permits and even encourages great variation in the way it is pursued and that, moreover, may be endorsed by a society in such a way as to assure toleration and even support for those who do not wish to pursue it in any manner.

These remarks are intended to convey fundamental sympathy with libertarianism and with its preference for diversity and its abhorrence of monolithic social orders. The ways in which I regard libertarianism as deficient should become clear as the argument of the book unfolds.

III

A society will prosper, so far as this is determined internally, if two conditions are met: it must create sufficient occasions for people to have the validating experiences; and those experiences must satisfy - they must be felt to give point to a system in which sacrifices make sense, if at all, as necessary in order to sustain the experiences.

The first condition doesn't necessarily require universalization of the focal value. This depends on the intentions of the system. Aristotle did not envisage a city in which everyone had intellectual virtue and devoted his time to leisurely contemplation. He spoke instead of a life of leisure for the few who were capable of it, and a life of toil for the rest in order that the conditions for leisure might be produced. Consumption, on the other hand, is a focal value that we are committed to universalizing. Marked inequalities are a sign of failure of the system. Most will hold that the aspiration to universalize is morally superior. But a society, such as that envisaged by Aristotle, that intends only a confined enjoyment of its validating experiences may nevertheless be highly stable. Those to whom the value is not intended to be distributed must have compensatory benefits, to assure enthusiasm for what is essentially a supporting role. Stability is further assured by their adopting the focal value as their own, and finding reason for enabling others to enjoy it while they are excluded from it in the fact that the system creates real approximations to its idealized character types, peoples the place with heroes.

Failure to satisfy these two conditions underlies the new revolutionary orientation of many people in the affluent countries. Their ambivalence is sometimes explained as a result of their being simultaneously involved in two revolutions.[4] The first, an industrial revolution, is marked by emphasis on work and success and focuses on creation of material amenity. Its final stage would consist in universalization of material values that are currently distributed unevenly. On the international level, this refers to the problem of minimizing discrepancies between affluent and impoverished nations. Within affluent nations, it refers to the problem of enabling minority groups, in particular blacks, to share in the affluence that the system bestows on others. But many of those who are emphatic beneficiaries of the system experience the emptiness of affluence and are searching for new values and lifestyles. Whatever direction the search takes, it is at least marked by rejection of the system. This rejection and search for new forms constitutes a post-industrial revolution.

Many who are involved in the second revolution nevertheless sense the importance of universalizing the values associated with the first. Ambivalence results, since the values to be universalized are precisely the ones found to be hollow. Although the point of intersection of the two revolutions is their common rejection of the system, they arrive at this point from opposed premises. The one rejects the system because it doesn't work; the other finds it most inadequate when in its own terms it works very well.

It is probably a misuse of words to speak of a post-industrial revolution in this connection. The individuals referred to conceive the system under which they live as brought to a focus around the value of consumption. Being peculiarly favoured members of the system, abundant validating experiences have been available to them. But the experiences haven't validated. They have had extensive opportunity to do the things the doing of which would make sense of their lives within the prevailing arrangement of affairs, if anything would, and have experienced the opportunities as senseless. It is rather more serious than just not being satisfied, since, given the accepted model, paradigmatic experiences of consuming put the system itself to a test. Although the problem is intensely personal, it implicates a world.

The two revolutions, then, are prompted by sensed failure of society to

4 K. Keniston, 'You Have to Grow Up in Scarsdale to Know How Bad Things Really Are,' *New York Times*, 27 April 1969.

satisfy the two-mentioned conditions for success of a social system. The industrial revolution is stymied by failure to distribute the focal value fairly, which means failure to create sufficient occasions for people generally to have the validating experiences. The post-industrial revolution arises from failure of those experiences to satisfy, to lend significance to the system that grounds them.

A society that fails in either of these two ways is likely to undergo changes, but the manner in which the changes occur and the clarity of purpose they exhibit will vary, depending on whether the underlying problem is failure to distribute the focal value adequately or its not seeming valuable to those who experience it. When the value is not fairly distributed, and this failing is felt to be irremediable within the established order, the conditions for violent attack on the system are present and the revolutionary energy in the society will enjoy considerable clarity of purpose. In this case there is something recognizable that the disadvantaged want and sense they are deprived of.

When the problem is created by widespread failure of the focal value to validate the system to those to whom it is available, a measure of pointless violence may ensue, but the larger effect will be the sorts of changes that follow upon ossification. For in these circumstances the system loses vitality. Life is withdrawn from it and it continues to function only as a pointless rite. Experimentation with new lifestyles begins in the interstices of the system. The hope for a happy issue rests with the prospect that energy withheld from established practices will fasten to some of the experiments, so that they prosper and form the nucleus around which a new order grows.

Alienation, an overworked term in the literature of social criticism, has an application to the circumstances just described. Imagine that a person has a fairly clear model of the society in which he lives. He sees it as organized around some focal value, perceives its institutions in terms of their role in supporting or defeating that value, identifies the character types that the system idealizes, and grasps the significance of the activities that are the source of the society's validating experiences – that is, realizes that these must validate it if anything would. People don't often comprehend their society in these respects with great clarity. Rather, they simply acquire a feeling for the kind of world they inhabit by having grown up in it. In these circumstances, discovery that the activities that should validate the system are pointless will leave them with a deep sense of being alienated. The experience is profound because the established social order *is* our reality. To find that we can neither identify with it nor lend our energy to it is to find ourself cut off from that one base we are bound to regard as home.

IV

Alienation, more than any other reaction to our situation, creates desire to experiment with new lifestyles. That the system is self-destructive and undirected are circumstances that elicit concern about the future. A person may have this concern, but because he finds the present sweet may not be strongly motivated to act on it. Alienation sweeps away contentment and transforms abstract concern about the future into a pressing personal problem. But, equally, perceiving that the established order is self-destructive and largely undirected may objectify what would otherwise be a merely private discontent. The problem is also social, and a first step toward its solution is discovery of a focal value around which a compelling image of the future can be erected. The following pages are an attempt to define that focal value and to indicate some of the main features of the image of the future it suggests.

CHAPTER TWO

Responsibility and the environment

Social critics often represent technology as an evil force responsible for many of our deep-rooted problems, thus reversing a long-standing acceptance of it as a saviour. Both views are wrong in the same way that it is wrong to credit or blame the knife used to carve a roast – it did the work well or poorly, but credit or blame goes to the one who took it up.[1] Typically, technology is a tool at the service of large corporations and governments. Underlying its use is a pervasive motivation to manipulate people and things for the creation and satisfaction of human wants. An adequate estimate of technology must be tied to a view of the manner in which this willingness to manipulate expresses itself, and of whether large corporations and governments have a predominantly active or passive role.

When an active role is stressed, the key factor is taken to be either the desire of those who possess economic power to maximize profits or that of those who possess political power to maximize economic growth as measured by gross national product. These are but two ways of looking at the same process, first from the corporations' side, then from that of government. The consumer is seen as passive and manipulated, acted upon, technology as the tool used for this purpose.

Changing the emphasis, one may see the system as consumer-oriented. Now the corporations and governments are servants of the consumer and technology

1 It is of course true that particular technologies create their own imperatives. A library that computerizes its 'retrieval system' imposes a new pattern of use by borrowers. And I also believe that current 'advanced' technologies have certain common features that produce effects on the people whose lives are somewhat structured by them: effects in the way of distinctive living patterns and in character structure. So we may speak of technology 'doing' things to us, and we do find reason for condemning some of those things. Consequently technology isn't entirely passive. But these facts are compatible with recognition that people or organizations control the technology, cause it to be developed in specific ways, and decide to use it in specific ways. *Therefore*, it is a mistake to represent technology as the villain or the saviour of the piece.

is the device by which they are enabled to sense and satisfy his autonomous preferences.

Or the manipulated-manipulator relationship, in either direction, may be dropped in favour of the view that producers and consumers are active, willing partners in one integrated system. In this case the dominant purpose technology serves is maintenance and growth of the system itself: more profits, more goods, more consumption, and more and more advanced technology.

However the scenario is written, so that capitalist manipulators lurk in the wings or all is quite impersonal and steely, innocent except in its outcome, there is one constant feature. The momentous consequences of the system's operation aren't intended or even foreseen by those whose actions give rise to them. Thus, so far as the aim is to maximize profit, the decisions that shape events will be sensitive to considerations that have implications for the entries on profit and loss statements and tax forms, but insensitive to those humanly significant considerations that lack such implications. When what makes the donkey go is the carrot at the end of the stick tied to his neck, the colour orange looms large in his experience, but he doesn't discriminate between blues and greens. Similarly, if the main business is to consume, or to maximize profits or GNP, the impact of decisions on the physical environment, human character, and non-economic institutions isn't brought into focus but is cast into a murky background within which discriminations are not made.

As a result, what the system intends to accomplish isn't nearly as important as what it accomplishes unintentionally. It is myopic, nearly blind. In one sense this is not a recent development. Almost two centuries ago Hegel developed a theory of history that gave indirection a central place. The unintended consequences of our actions, he held, tend to be of greater historical importance than the intended ones. Our aims are narrow but our deeds ramify widely, and the really significant events in human history escape everyone's intentions.[2]

But in Hegel's day the pace of change was much slower. The fact that while intending one thing we simultaneously accomplish another, and that world-history is the accumulation of these unintended results, seemed quaint and amusing. Now, with a quicker pace, more massive consequences, and greater capability for self-destruction, we must seek our amusement elsewhere. Hegel believed, moreover, in an imminent providence, Reason, which assured that however narrow and selfish the aims of individuals may be, their deeds are unwittingly rational and beneficent in a world-historical perspective – Adam Smith's invisible hand applied to world history. Today there is better basis for

2 G.W.F. Hegel, *Lectures on the Philosophy of History*, trans. J. Sibree (London, 1857), pp. 28-34.

a reversal of the position. We may find the intentions of individuals laudable in the extreme, but what they unintentionally build seems none the less frightening.

II

A model of the future gains its contemporary relevance by incorporating responses to the large human issues created by myopic application of technology. Three of these issues concern the impact of an advanced technology on the environment, on the traditional community, and on the significance and availability of work and leisure. In each area uncontrolled technology has led to massive problems and unprecedented opportunities. (1) It has brought impressive capability of using the environment for satisfaction of genuine human needs and has made available a treasure trove of devices which, intelligently used, would improve the quality of life. Equally, it has squandered our natural resources, fouled our air, and polluted our waterways. (2) Owing largely to increased mobility – including mobility of attention made possible by centralized mass communications – it has prompted development of unique individual capacities while destroying traditional communities and failing to introduce the ingredients on the basis of which a new form of community might establish itself. (3) And, finally, labour-saving devices, in particular automated production processes, have put within our grasp the leisure society. But they have also made work for many people an inane exercise, have created unemployment for others, and have left still others with large amounts of leisure they are unequipped to take advantage of, so that lives of boredom and felt triviality replace lives of toil.

Each issue is a nest of interrelated problems to which much thought has been given. Through the various solutions suggested there run common themes. As a result, in connection with each issue we can associate a pair of opposed attitudes. (1) Thought about environmental problems is divided into two camps: some stress the need to humanize technology, others would have us go as far as possible toward dispensing with it – which takes the form of a plea for 'returning to nature.' (2) In thinking about the dissolution of traditional community, some welcome it, as involving liberation of the individual from deadening group conformity, while others seek institutional reforms and urban designs that will either restore it or create a new form that adapts old values to modern conditions. (3) The issue created by the possibility of a leisure society leads some to recommend restoring human significance to work, and others to recommend automating industry so that human labour will not be necessary and the great majority of people might enjoy lives of leisure.

Despite widespread acceptance of their gravity, these issues are seldom discussed in the same context. One reason perhaps is that in its technical aspects each is associated with a different academic discipline. The set of mind peculiar to each is not such as to make a representative of it comfortable with the terminology and concerns of the other two. Thus, serious discussion of environmental problems has a natural home in biology and ecology. The threat to traditional community is in the main subject-matter for sociologists and city-planners. And the issues of work and leisure involve the competence and orientation of economists in a distinctive way.

Interrelationships among the three issues, however, make it desirable to overcome their isolation from one another. Apart from the fact that a model of the future should respond coherently to all three – a result that cannot be assured so long as they are discussed in isolation – typical responses share assumptions that ought not to go unquestioned. These responses fall into patterns that reflect underlying philosophical orientations which, while the issues are isolated from one another, are neither noticed nor criticized. Thus the comforting delusion is established that the issues present nothing more than technical problems, requiring discovery of techniques or schemes for accomplishing non-controversial results, and presenting no challenge to underlying values and tacit world-views. A comforting delusion, since it leads to structuring the issues in the way those concerned are familiar with, so that much of the difficulty is kept from their view, and they are enabled to regard their biases as obvious and assured truths.

The patterns exemplified by responses to the three issues may be distinguished by their degree of attachment to the past. Those who, in the face of massive environmental problems, think primarily of minimizing reliance on technology in effect contemplate a return to a condition that Western man once enjoyed but has given up in his enthusiasm for technological progress. It is a natural extension of this theme, when confronted by the anonymity of urban life and the moribund state of small towns, to search for ways of restoring traditional community or to advocate some latter-day adaptation. And similar 'conservatism' is reflected in the view that rather than push for greater mechanization and automation of production we should try to make work itself humane.[3]

From the other side, to speak of humanizing technology, to relegate community to the past and stress individualized lifestyles, and to endorse the economic efficiency that holds promise of a leisure-oriented society is to be 'progressive.' These attitudes exhibit considerably less regard for traditional values and greater willingness to build the future around new elements made possible by scientific and technological advance.

3 These themes are interwoven in an influential document, 'A Blueprint for Survival,' published in *The Ecologist*, II, no 1 (January 1972), especially pp. 14-17.

The progressive and conservative orientations find their philosophical rationale in sets of ideas that have a long history. One set forms the tradition of individualism, the other of wholism. Unfortunately, whatever merit these sets of ideas may have had in the past, neither serves well when brought to bear on the prominent issues of our day. This view, for which I shall argue in the following pages, poses a challenge to develop an orientation that more adequately illuminates the issues. There are strong reasons for doubting that we should seek to minimize dependence on technology or to humanize it; to create a leisure-oriented society or one in which people find the core meanings of life in work; to restore traditional community or to intensify individuality and liberate the individual from the rest of mankind.

III

The environmental crisis has been effectively publicized. People have learned that conditions met first-hand – when they drive to work and choke on the air, walk in the country and find filthy water where in their youth clear streams flowed – obtain world-wide. We read of the diminishing numbers of wild animals in Africa, of species of fish and animals that have recently become extinct or are in danger of doing so, of the air in Tokyo. Signs along the shore of Lake Geneva warn that the water is unfit for swimming. Other lakes, until recently brimming with fish and aquatic animals, are now incapable of supporting any life at all. The Mediterranean, because of its nearly landlocked situation, has been devastated by oil, industrial waste, and sewage; a swimmer has been estimated to stand a one-in-seven chance of catching a disease through sewage discharge. Only one-tenth of Tel Aviv's beaches are fit for swimming. Recently, half of Genoa's beaches were closed because of sewage pollution. Industrial pollution in the Berre lagoon (Marseilles) and bay of Muggia (Trieste) has destroyed almost all of the fish. The canals of Amsterdam are connected to the toilets of Amsterdam, and every evening a change of water level flushes them into waterways that carry Dutch defecation to the North Sea. At many points, the northern Adriatic is a cesspool. The dates when many of our natural resources shall finally be used up have been calculated. Ominous long-term effects of radioactive fallout and other resultants of the uses to which nuclear technology is put have been discovered. We are told that pollution levels in the oceans themselves are rising alarmingly. And to this is added a projection of population growth that forces us to take seriously the barbarous concept of 'people pollution.'

Some who warn of these dangers are called apostles of doom.[4] Others are

4 J. Maddox, *The Doomsday Syndrome* (London, 1972).

said to be radicals who magnify the environmental crisis to gain sympathy for their politics. Not everyone is reduced to despair. Nevertheless, no one denies that the problem is serious. Many of the conditions that support human life on the planet are now precarious and many living species are in jeopardy. During the past twenty years the magnitude of environmental problems has increased to such an extent that we face a qualitatively new situation of massive proportions.

Concern prompted by awareness of the crisis gives rise to two opposed attitudes. One holds that environmental problems result from a too hasty application of technology, not from technology as such or from the fact that it is advanced or pervasive. Thus, an insecticide for eliminating a crop-devouring insect is discovered. Instantly it is put to use. Only then are its disastrous side-effects noticed. Diagnosis: they went into production too quickly, before learning enough about the chemical. Cure: use the scientific techniques by which the insecticide was produced for discovering as well the full range of side-effects of its use, and defer putting it to use until this knowledge is gained. The problem isn't too much science and technology but too little – and too late. Since the side-effects of interest are those with implications for the quality of human life, this attitude toward environmental problems leads to stress on the importance of *humanizing* technology.[5]

The second attitude opposes technology as such. The relation between the two parallels that between two attitudes toward alcoholism. One person decides on total abstinence, another seeks intelligent use – drinking, to paraphrase Aristotle, 'with the right persons, at the right times.' Obviously, no one recommends total abstinence with respect to technology – even chimpanzees fashion tools for scooping edible ants from their nests. But there is scope for a cut-back in our commitment to its characteristic contemporary manifestations. If we refer to those who adopt this perspective as forming a 'back to nature' movement, we are thinking of a direction and an emphasis not an envisaged ideal state of affairs.

To sense when reflecting on environmental problems en masse that we have relied too much on science and technology in ordering our lives is to sense that there has been too much making and consuming, not that we haven't been clever enough about it. As a result, one whose orientation is anti-technology need not place as high a priority on recycling as do those who stress a human-

5 B. Commoner, *Science and Survival* (London, 1966). Commoner couples this with stress on the importance of an 'informed citizenry': 'Science can reveal the depth of this crisis, but only social action can resolve it. Science can now serve society by exposing the crisis of modern technology to the judgement of all mankind. Only this judgement can determine whether the knowledge that science has given us shall destroy humanity or advance the welfare of man' (p. 132).

ized technology. But since the orientation is essentially negative not a great deal can be said about its positive application. In general it idealizes a simpler style of life and evokes images of earlier times when life was more rural, less complex and hurried, closer to nature.

IV

Despite the sharp contrast between stress on humanizing and on minimizing dependence on technology, the two views share a questionable assumption. This is reflected in the current understanding of what an 'environmental problem' is. The 'environment' is the collection of physical, external circumstances that form the setting for our lives. It is distinguished from nature in general in that it is not a passive backdrop, but is that part of the natural setting with which we interact, that facilitates and obstructs our activity. Identification of some natural conditions as forming an 'environmental problem' has the effect of locating the difficulty in the unsuitability of those conditions for human uses. An environmental problem arises when, owing to our neglect or carelessness, nature becomes less useful to us in some respect. Thus, in discussion of environmental problems one occasionally meets the glib but false saying that man is the only animal who fouls his own nest – which depends for its relevance on the assumption that it is the fitness of the environment for human uses that is at issue.

But does the whole basis for concern about a polluted stream, say, arise from such consequences as that it has become less suitable for swimming, fishing, boating, and the like? Is it the stream in its role of forming an environment for human life that ought to be our sole concern? At first glance this seems not only correct but self-evident. We are no doubt influenced by the moral tradition that has been dominant in the West during the past 350 years. That tradition has been anthropocentric in the sense that it has defined all fundamental ethical categories – right, good, duty, justice – with reference to man, so that they are not applicable to events and objects out of relationship with human life.

Familiar issues, however, are difficult to square with the anthropocentric assumption. A proposed dam promises to change the ecology of an area so that a variety of fish found only in the river affected by the dam will become extinct. How is concern about their survival to be explained? Typically discussion centres on the utility of the fish and of a river that contains them. If the river is largely inaccessible, the conservationist may fall back on an appeal to the importance of allowing it to remain in its natural state so that an occasional person may walk its banks, knowing and enjoying the realization that the fish are there. But if the premise is that we are trying to preserve an environment for human use, this is plainly a weak defence. Few will walk the banks, fewer will know the fish are there, and few of those who know will care. No doubt some priority can be attached to preservation of the river in its natural state, in light of the exotic preferences of a handful of people, but scarcely enough to raise the utility of preservation above that of building the dam.

That despite his manner of arguing his case the conservationist is not fundamentally concerned about human uses is shown by his subsequent appeal to the future. Grant, we are told, that present interests are predominantly on the side of building the dam; nevertheless, to bow to these interests is to deprive all future generations of an irreplaceable amenity. The attempt now is to portray those interested in preservation as in the majority, those interested in dams as a rapacious minority – since we may presume that the future generations will outnumber the present. But this ignores the fact that the distribution of preferences in future generations is likely to be roughly what it is now. Worse, generations born after the fish are gone may not even feel deprived, since they may not learn of such species ever having existed.

This may be generalized to cover many of the concerns discussed under the heading of 'environmental problems.' When we think merely in terms of utility, of human uses and preferences, adding them up, each to count for one, we are unable to make a compelling case for doing many of the things that we attempt to justify by talking about cleaning up or preserving the environment. Often more actual interests are served by a polluted stream than by a clean one, by killing off a species of fish than by preserving it, by developing a wilderness area as a vacation site.

Environmentalists should be embarrassed by such facts. In our intellectual climate, the only compelling ground on which to oppose 'development' involves appeal to human benefits and needs. That this line of argument fails should be faced.[6] When it is faced, only two courses are open: one can give up the conservationist position, resting confidence in the appeal to human benefits and needs; or hold firmly to that position, but seek a more adequate theoretical basis for it.

6 Of course in any case the conservationist himself has a preference for (or 'interest' in) keeping the environment in its natural state. One might think, then, the issue is wrongly formulated here – that what is at stake is whether the conservationists' interests or those of developers will be given priority. This is correct as far as it goes. But the question raised in the text concerns the principle on which the dispute between conservationists and developers should be settled. Should we adopt as our goal that of maximizing satisfaction of preferences or needs? Or should we hold that there are some conditions that are valuable – preservation of threatened species, for example – even if they don't lead to 'the greatest good for the greatest number'? In the latter case, one may well ask how we find out that such conditions are indeed valuable. This matter is discussed at length in the Afterword.

V

In one sense, everyone opposes exploitation. A use of the natural surroundings that is careless of the needs of others, that creates conditions that make the lives of future generations less tolerable, is obviously exploitative, a misuse. The ethical categories that cover the case are justice and fairness. In taking from the environment more than our fair share, leaving little for those who follow, we do them an injustice. By using up amenities they might have enjoyed, we allocate to ourselves freedoms to which they have an equal claim.

In a deeper sense, the assumption that the natural surroundings are there for our use, even when subjected to the constraint that we not take more than our fair share, is itself exploitative. In the first sense, exploitation raises issues regarding the appropriate relationship of men with men, and of the present with future generations. In the second sense, the deeper issue of man's relationship with nature is posed. Those who respond to environmental problems by proposing that technology be humanized accept the underlying exploitative perspective and ask only that we be fair about it. Those who argue that if we are to survive we must substantially withdraw our commitment to technology assume that exploitation is the only possible relationship, but that to avoid the bad consequences it introduces a self-denying policy of non-interference should be adopted. They don't recommend anything positive.

We require an alternative to this exploitative perspective: an understanding of the stance toward nature that it involves - beyond the bald statement that natural things have value as such, independently of human needs - and of the kinds of action upon the environment that are consonant with it. At first glance, the key concept of ecology, that of a balanced ecological community or ecosystem, suggests such an alternative. An ecosystem is a collection of colonies of various living things, along with natural features and objects, all found in a geographically delimitable space and mutually interacting so as to form a viable whole. If the location is a forest floor, the community may consist of a number of colonies of various species of animals and plants, a pine needle bed, characteristically moist air, the configuration of the land, etc. These features, living and inert, will be in some measure of balance: in their active relationships with one another each element will maintain and be maintained by the overall scheme. In the long run, what survives is the scheme as a whole, not necessarily the elements. Thus, ecological balance is instanced when lightning starts a fire in a stand of conifers and fire thorns sprout in the sun-drenched ground surrounding the charred trunks.

The ecological perspective prompts an active relationship with nature radically different from that prevalent in the West during the past few centuries. The effect of emphasizing self-maintaining processes of ecosystems is to project on to nature a tendency to achieve and sustain desirable states. This reintroduces into our world-view the attribution of purposiveness to nature, which has been unpopular since the seventeenth century when Aristotelian teleology was discredited by modern physical science. That ecosystems tend toward stability is just one fact alongside others. The ecological perspective is the result of taking a certain attitude toward the fact. After one has identified the processes through which the tendency toward stability expresses itself, these are accepted as desirable and an attitude toward nature and human society is adopted that reflects this valuation.

Two examples should suffice. (1) We can associate with the self-maintaining tendency of any ecosystem an optimum population for each of the various colonies of living things that it contains. This 'law' points in two directions. In the ordinary course of events, the system tends to maintain the colonies at the optimum level. But also, when circumstances ('unnaturally') cause a colony to increase beyond the optimum, the health of the colony and of the ecosystem as a whole are disrupted. (2) Any ecosystem tends toward complexity and variety: its self-maintaining capability is enhanced by incorporation of numerous colonies and numerous forms of interaction among them, so that the balance is maintained by an extensive network of interreacting processes. This 'law' has two comparable faces. In the ordinary course of events an ecosystem will incorporate increasing variety and complexity until an optimum state has been reached. Also, if ('unnaturally') the variety and complexity are reduced or suppressed, as when man interferes by introducing pesticides, the self-maintaining capability of the system is threatened. The optima alluded to by such laws define the climax state of the ecosystem.

These laws lead to two features of the attitude toward nature inherent in the ecological perspective. First, they prompt a bias toward non-interference with natural processes, an attitude of laissez-faire vis-à-vis nature, based on confidence that the fundamental tendency is toward desirable outcomes. The presupposition is that climax states are *good*. Second, since human life is not possible without extensive interaction with natural things, the laws suggest principles that should guide those interactions. In the present case, these are that complexity and variety of ecosystems should not be wantonly reduced, and that optimum population levels for the colonies that form an ecosystem should not be artificially suppressed or exceeded.

The resulting stance toward nature is thus diametrically opposed to an exploitative one. The characteristic feature of the latter is that the natural objects with which one interacts are treated as utilities and nothing more. I impose my will on them in the interest of satisfying a need of my own. It is material for my satisfaction. The initiative and purpose are on my side. Under the influence of the ecological perspective, with attribution of initiative and directedness to nature itself, I place myself instead in a *custodial* role: either passively allowing the beneficent processes to occur, not interfering, or adapting my activity to them in the interest of helping them along. In so doing, I put myself at the service of processes that have their direction independently of me, and that have an initiative of their own for achieving the states they are directed toward. Thus, the attitude of standing astride and dominating nature is replaced by one of acceptance and of caring for something that is beyond oneself. From being an exploiter, man becomes a custodian.

The ecological perspective suffers, however, from two serious limitations. It does not integrate the human world with the ecosystems that constitute the natural realm, and stability or self-maintenance is a too limited norm for ecosystems that are conceived as including man.

Ecosystems are in effect subsystems incorporated into an overarching ecosphere that as a whole exhibits the characteristics found in local systems, most especially the tendency toward stability. Man, along with everything else on the planet, exists within the ecosphere and is subject to its laws. But just as the various ecosystems, when thought of in relation with man, are conceived as *environments*, so the ecosphere itself is conceived as a total environment for the human world. These self-maintaining systems are not comprehended as including man. He is not grasped as a natural element within them but is seen as standing outside. Lip-service is often paid to the presence of man in nature, but this is merely platitudinous, since no account is given of his distinctive role there. To stress the importance of our respecting the principles by which ecosystems maintain themselves is but to recommend, in effect, that we negotiate a modus vivendi with them, so that our presence doesn't work to their disadvantage – a very different thing from reaching the conception of a community in which men and other living things coexist, and in which our presence has positive significance.

This limitation makes the second inevitable. Stability, self-maintenance, is a plausible norm for a community of interacting living things from which men are excluded. We need ask no more of a woodlot removed from human habitation than that its self-maintaining mechanisms be permitted to operate so that it may eventually reach a climax that is 'natural.' Each of the living constituents develops in the way its unimpeded life processes prompt it to when found in a setting in which all of the others are doing so as well. The collective result is an accommodation of each to the rest, and stability is the tendency of the accommodation first to be achieved and then to persist. There are enormous theoretical difficulties in the way of defending this accommodation as being 'natural,' but almost no one fails to sense that it is and that because it is it is good. I would suggest, however, that what prompts this instinctive response – that the climax state of an ecosystem is a natural state and being natural is the state it ought to reach and maintain – is our perception of its unforced character. Since it is the accommodation negotiated by the constituents of the system under conditions that allow each to develop according to its own principles, we see it as the *fair* result. The freedom of each colony to proliferate, and of each individual to grow, is confined only by the constraint that the others be left free to do likewise. Positive evaluation of climax states and of the mechanisms that lead up to them reflects our instinct for primitive justice: tacit acceptance of the principle of equal freedom, that each should be free to develop in his own way, provided only that he does not interfere with a like attempt by others. We project what is for many a self-evident principle of social organization on to ecosystems from which man is excluded.

But once man is introduced into the ecosystem, not simply as a meddler or as an outside agent giving a boost to the self-maintaining processes, but as another natural element with his own exigencies and principles of development, the norm of self-maintenance becomes problematic. If we conceive his influence as solely custodial, as supporting a climax state that would have formed the goal of the system had man been excluded from it, we aren't really conceiving him as an interactive element within the system. Addition of any significant new element to an ecosystem changes the character of the mutual accommodation that forms its climax state, toward the achievement and maintenance of which the system tends. An ecosystem that genuinely includes man gains thereby a new direction, new tendencies, a new climax. Otherwise his presence is not recognized, and our view of the system is unnatural.

What man brings is creativity, a tendency to conceive values – admirable possibilities of material – and a capability of shaping objects and situations so that those possibilities are realized. Any ecosystem in which creativity does not show itself does not include man as an integral element. In evolutionary terms, creativity is the outcome of a long course of development in which man lost most of his highly specific programmed responses, instincts. Other living things have organically grounded capabilities that are fairly determinate. They respond in generally predictable, specific ways, for which we can account by reference to the organism itself, on one side, and facilitating and obstructing features of its environment, on the other. Given a comparable set of facilitating and obstructing features, man always has more options. His environment and make-up don't confine him to anything like the same degree. Consequently, his responses are inevitably to a very considerable extent selective. The selection reflects an estimate of the relative values of the alternatives, and the subsequent action is creative in that it undertakes to give reality to a valued objective, freely chosen.

VI

What will be our view of our relationship with nature if we overcome the limitations of the ecological perspective? The predominantly custodial role to which the latter relegates man results from failure to apprehend him as existing within nature and developing in that setting in distinctive ways. The exploitative perspective assigns man a role in which creativity is acknowledged but in such a way that he sets himself against nature. An integral view would direct our value-creating capability toward nature in the interest of perfecting the whole that we along with it form. A person's primary sense in the presence of nature would then become that of being *responsible*.[7] His not apprehending

7 The term 'responsibility' recommends itself in this connection, despite its often being employed in senses not intended here, because of two strong connotations it frequently carries. First, particularly in locutions in which the content of one's responsibility is not specified ('He is responsible,' 'I am a responsible person'), there is a connotation of personal commitment voluntarily (responsibly) undertaken. The idea is that of a person's autonomously shouldering a burden, making it his because he *decides* that it ought to be, or that it would be best if it were, done; and decides moreover that it would be best that *he* do it. Sartre's use of the French equivalent of the term capitalizes especially on this connotation. Second, 'responsibility,' in many locutions, connotes something approaching causal efficacy: 'I am responsible for having done that' = 'I did it.'

These connotations are relevant because I am attempting to identify a stance toward nature that has two features. A 'responsible' person accepts that (1) in his interactions with nature he may well affect great changes, and this is not *as such* objectionable, and (2) what those changes are – the state in which he leaves the world – matters to him *finally* (that is, it matters to him simply in virtue of what it is, not in virtue of what it implies for him or his kind, its effects).

The first feature distinguishes the stance to which I am applying the term 'responsibility' from that which I have called 'custodial.' The second feature marks the distinction from 'exploitation.' 'Responsibility,' through the first-mentioned connotation (personal commitment voluntarily undertaken) is intended to carry the sense of this second feature, particularly with the understanding that the final or intrinsic values a responsible person ascribes to nature are not objectively there in the way rocks and straw are, but are imputed to nature in a creative act. 'Responsibility,' through the second-mentioned connotation, causal efficacy, is intended to carry the sense of the first feature.

It should be noted that it does not follow straightaway, from the claim that final values are imputed to nature in a creative act rather than found there in the way we find rocks and straw, that any imputation of value to nature is as warranted as any other. There may well be 'criteria for success' in creativity, and I believe there are. Frank Lloyd Wright's house, Fallingwater, is paradigmatic of a responsible treatment of nature. It would be ludicrous to hold that any other manner of exploiting the ground on which it stands would have been equally successful.

nature as an environment with which he interacts as an outside agent would be expressed in the sense of being continuous with it, of being an important element in a whole that includes natural things as well as the human world. The sense of responsibility is a stance one takes within this whole. The dominant tone is that the whole itself has value that is both in jeopardy and susceptible of enhancement.

Human creativity implies a unique competence to bring value to the whole and to preserve values attributed to it. Inevitably, this involves altering natural things and application of techniques and of technology in the process. But the context in which this occurs is not bifurcated, does not place man on one side and nature on the other as a domain of material used for his satisfaction. The technology rather is introduced as the principal tool by which man makes his distinctive difference. As a result, the alterations need not be exploitative or consist in 'interfering' with nature, any more than we can apply these terms to a sculptor's activity chiselling a block of marble. He acts on valued possibilities seen in the material itself, its form, texture, and grain, and is prompted by the sense that to bring those possibilities to life is not merely to do something for himself, relieve an itch or produce a commodity, but is to do something appropriate for the material as well and thereby for the whole in which he and the material are found.

Responsibility involves identifying with that whole, attributing value to it, and grasping the significance of one's life in terms of one's manner of relating with it. To be responsible is to hold fast to the sense that the important feature of one's activity in relation with the natural surroundings is the state they are left in as a result, not the state one brings oneself into. It is no more responsible to resolve to act so that one's own presence is not felt and not shown than it is for the individual or the race to deal with the natural surroundings as nothing more than amenities and resources for development. The former perspective signifies unwillingness to take up one's distinctive responsibility within the whole, the latter failure to turn one's efforts outward.

The analogy with sculpture may be extended: the sculptor senses personal responsibility to create, to exercise his talent, and also aesthetic responsibility to respect his material, to be guided by his sense of what is appropriate for it to become, not what a dealer, a customer, or his 'public' want. The first form of irresponsibility corresponds with the custodial role; the second with exploitation. Neither acknowledges man's continuity with the rest of nature, the first because it does not accept man as man but reduces him to a servant, the second because the active role it attributes to man is divisive.

The stance of responsibility implies no solutions to particular environmental problems, any more than does the attitude that we should humanize technology or withdraw our commitment to it. Just as these latter orientations only establish prima facie emphases and priorities but don't dictate specific responses to concrete problems, so the view that we want a *responsible* technology only suggests a general conception of its appropriate role in our interactions with the natural surroundings. But if it were in our power to choose the orientation in terms of which critical decisions regarding application of technology are made, we would be wise to pass over strident custodians and exploiters and seek out people in whom there are stirrings of responsibility.

CHAPTER THREE

Dissolution of community

One of the profound effects of our commitment to technology has been the dissolution of traditional community. The small, self-contained settlements of the past, with their solidarity and insularity, are either submerged in larger urban complexes marked by more individualistic lifestyles or else are drying up and dying out - younger inhabitants moving to the big city when they reach the age of consent, leaving behind clusters of old-folks' homes on the fringes of civilization. And in the cities themselves, small enclaves, traditional neighbourhoods, are undergoing similar absorption or atrophy.

It is not disappearance of these small places as such, but elimination of the collective lifestyles they incorporated, that provokes thought and, occasionally, concern. In one account, *Gemeinschaft* is seen as replaced by *Gesellschaft*. In another, the face-to-faceness and wholeness of group life in villages and neighbourhoods are said to have been supplanted by impersonalization and fragmentation.

Some, stressing the unwholesome features of small places and impressed by the vitality and excitement of urban life, welcome the development and heap scorn on expressions of nostalgia for real villages. Others, impressed by what they take to be enduring values sustained by these places, but absent from highly urbanized areas, seek ways of either recovering traditional community or creating a modern version, adapted to the forces responsible for eroding the historic form.[1]

The issue created by dissolution of community receives less publicity than does the environmental crisis, and groups of sociologists and planners don't issue manifestoes and form clubs for organizing a response to the issue and enlisting public support as do their counterparts in biology and ecology. In part,

1 To my mind, the most persuasive statements of the opposing points of view are those of Baker Brownell, *The Human Community* (New York, 1950), and Jane Jacobs, *The Death and Life of Great American Cities* (New York, 1961).

the reason is that not everyone concerned agrees there *is* an issue, other than that created by the need to put down those who think there is. And then the dissolution has been going on for so long that we take it for granted.

We may think of 'community' in two ways. As a kind of place or settlement – as when we speak of *the* traditional community, in which case villages and small towns come first to mind. Or, as a quality of life sustained by the stable relations among people settled together in the same place. Those relations exhibit 'community' to the extent they involve such features as a common purpose, self-identification with a common past, common concerns co-operatively pursued, mutual involvement in a common way of life. In referring to the dissolution of traditional community, I have both of these uses in mind: the disappearance of places – villages, small towns, neighbourhoods – in which community as a quality of life is typically found.

Those who lament the loss do so because they see value in these kinds of relationships among people, and in the bonds they establish. It is said that man is by nature a social animal, not merely in that he needs others to satisfy his wants but in that his nature is fulfilled and completed only by entering into community with others. And this philosophic estimate is sometimes supported by the psychological observation that adequate self-identification and self-esteem are best maintained if a person matures within the familiar, supportive environment of a genuine community. Looking outward to public benefits, some add that the inhabitants of a settlement are never so likely to maintain it adequately – its quality of life as well as its physical features – as when they relate with one another as a community and locate the central point of their existence in a life they lead together. It is at least true that loss of community has involved emergence of the idea that the public domain is a means for the enrichment of lives that find their main point within private spheres; there is an easy transition from this orientation to a practice of taking what one can from the public domain without regard for its resulting capability of meeting the needs of others. And, finally, it may be argued that there is a conceptual linkage between community and morality: that dissolution of community brings patterns of living that are inherently immoral. Here it is assumed that with loss of communal bonds the lives of detached individuals inevitably take on a quality of selfishness.

These considerations may or may not raise nostalgia for community to the level of a reasoned and defended perspective. But there can be no doubt that the sentiment is powerful or that the considerations mentioned describe the motivations of those affected by it. Pursuit of self-identification, desire for a deeply satisfying lifestyle, interest in a public domain that can be seen as intrinsically valuable, and search for a way of life that satisfies our sense of morality have prompted numerous communitarian experiments. Not least of these are the 'establishment' communities of communist countries. Rural and urban communes in China and collective farms in eastern Europe and Cuba involve hundreds of millions of people, a sizable percentage of the world population. Although in part these have been established for economic and political reasons, they are also inspired by the idea that a community lifestyle is more admirable than that prevalent in the individualistic cities of the West. Comparable experiments begun in Palestine at the beginning of the century have proliferated. In the West, long-standing religious communes prosper as never before, so much so that some now face the problem of whether to admit young people who have no interest in their religion but are attracted by the communitarian social organization of the farms. In the cities, communal families motivated by a communitarian ideal are often found. In some areas the countryside is dotted with similar communes based on farming and distinguished by their integration of the settings of work and family life.

Evidently, then, if there is a strong element of nostalgia in the ideal of community, nevertheless it is considerably more than a relic of the past but is a vital present force. To mistakenly suppose that all of the energies of the present are running in one direction, toward individualistic lifestyles, has the misleading effect of representing the 'urbanist' as the realist in the dispute about community, and his opponent as anachronistic.

Although enthusiasm for community is strong and growing, the forces that work against it seem distinctively contemporary. The reason is that they are associated with an advanced technology. With each technological advance community is placed in further jeopardy. New modes of transportation increase the individual's range, so that there is no one place in which the bulk of his activity is carried out. Developments in communication permit his mind and attention to range widely as well. And new production techniques isolate the sphere of work from family and neighbourhood, and even isolate workers from one another.

Defenders of the new lifestyles ushered in by dissolution of community see value in the greater freedom and individuality they exhibit. The other face of dissolution of community is liberation of the individual from the group. The typical inhabitant of an English manorial village during the middle ages may have had a vocabulary of only a few hundred words, and during his entire lifetime saw perhaps only a few hundred other human beings, almost all of whom were people very like himself in outlook, taste, and competence. We need look no farther than the most deprived slum dweller to learn that human sensitivity and intellect are capable of development far beyond that achieved by the mediaeval villager. This increased development of human capability is clearly desirable, whatever one may think of other losses along the way, and the new patterns of human relationship that result from our commitment to advanced technology are responsible for it.

The settlements that have replaced traditional communities – large urban complexes so diffuse that it is difficult to think of them as settlements at all – are beset with much-publicized, serious problems. But it is possible to argue that solution lies not in seeking to reintroduce community as a quality of life but in making the city work as a city, accepting the values of individuality and freedom as primary and building an environment in which technology enhances these values. This view parallels that which holds that we should seek solution to environmental problems in a humanized technology. Similarly, the partisan of community is likely to take the same negative attitude toward technology as do those ecologists who desire that it be not humanized but abandoned.

The issue is intensified by the plausibility of the values appealed to by the antagonists. Traditional communities sustained values whose disappearance we should lament. But the new order of human relationships replacing these communities brings conditions we should seek to retain. Anyone who would rather take a whole than a half loaf would be wise to hesitate before choosing his half.

II

Traditional community is a way of life. As such it is grounded in five traits of the practices of a people. Their life together is highly localized, exhibits continuity of acquaintance, is rooted to a place and a past, is continuous with nature, and has a public focus.[2] Dissolution of community has meant diffusion, discontinuity of acquaintance, rootlessness, discontinuity with nature, and privatization.

1 A person's round of life may be localized or diffuse. If we imagine that a round of life is the sum of a person's activities, and that each day repeats each preceding day so that he is constantly going the same round, then its scope will be the extent of the territory he ranges over each day. In traditional communities this territory was of course extremely confined. It is obvious that so far as it is possible to apply the idea of a round of life to our own situation, it is quite spread out. An airline pilot is an extreme case. More routinely vacationing away from home, commuting long distances to work, changing jobs frequently, sending children to consolidated schools at some distance from their neighbourhood or bussing them, are signs of diffusion.

2 The 'traditional community' described by means of these five traits is an ideal type. Perhaps the manorial village of mediaeval England is the closest approximation. In any case our own small villages are but distant cousins. And between the 'traditional community' and its idealized opposite – a non-community that would emphatically lack all five defining traits – lie the various forms of town and country environment that *we* inhabit: the inner city, suburbia, exurbia, etc.

Diffusion means transient populations. If we think of a settlement as a system of opportunities for leading a more or less complete life, diffusion means that it becomes a service centre. The opportunities are there, each fixed to a relatively permanent station within the settlement, and the populations pass through. They take up certain of the opportunities, then move on. In such circumstances individual rounds of life are diffused across settlements. Localization means, by contrast, that there is a match between the round of life and a particular settlement. People still speak of a specific place as being their 'home' and where they 'live,' but for very many this is an archaic manner of speech surviving from a time when people's lives were in fact tied to settlements.

Despite considerable diffuseness in rounds of life, it is still possible to speak of settlements because the opportunities these places offer cover most of the elements of what currently passes for a complete life. We have settlements in which no one is totally settled. A further development, which would signify disappearance of settlements themselves, would consist of specialization of the opportunities they offer. If one settlement became exclusively the place for sleeping, another for working, another for worshipping, etc., then none would actually be a settlement and we should say either that mankind had entered a post-settlement phase or else that it had evolved a global settlement. In any case, dissolution of traditional community does not consist in this development, but in diffusion of rounds of life across settlements.

If the full range of a person's life is confined to a particular place, it is likely that he will identify with it in a fairly complete way. But when his life is diffused across settlements, he is unlikely to identify with any one of them to the same extent. With this attenuation of the tie between the person and the settlement one of the principal motives for maintaining it as a settlement is weakened and conditions exist for its conversion into a specialized place where some particular human function is carried out.

2 A natural outcome of a number of people having settled their lives in the same, rather confined, locale is that they develop extensive continuity of acquaintance. The members of a nomadic tribe obviously move about much of the time, but since they move as a block their relationships with one another need not be affected by fluidity in their common relationships with outsiders. Their continuity of acquaintance means that through the various activities into which their round of life is articulated, again and again they confront the same individuals within the tribe. Their relations with outsiders are marked by considerable discontinuity of acquaintance. The relevant question is how far, in passing from eating to playing, to working, to resting, to worshipping, to governing, etc., a person confronts the same people.

Continuity of acquaintance does not presuppose a localized lifestyle. But confinement of many rounds of life to the same locale certainly makes it probable that extensive continuity of acquaintance will develop. When the two traits occur together we have the nucleus of our conception of a traditional community: a stable population brought into continuing contact with one another in a confined space. Here, two of the central connotations of 'community' are expressed: first, a place where a number of people have thoroughly settled their lives; second, a population, denizens who, because of the ways they interact with one another, are more than a loose group of people but form a corporate body.

The change from an earlier integration of the spheres of work and family life to the present separation of the two brought with it increased discontinuity of acquaintance. Moreover, one major function of neighbourhood is that of promoting continuity of acquaintance, particularly among children whose environment is beginning to reach beyond the home. Discontinuity of acquaintance is a major result of development of highly specialized functions in economic and social institutions. All of these changes – separation of the spheres of work and family life, disappearance of neighbourhood, and introduction of highly specialized tasks in economic and social institutions – have been prompted by our commitment to technology.

When urban critics make invidious comparisons between older, small-town lifestyles and those found in large cities, they often approve the 'face-to-faceness' of the former in contrast to the 'impersonality' of the latter. But impersonality is a feature of many face-to-face relationships, and it is possible to be friendly by post. Whether people confront one another face-to-face or not has little to do with the matter. What the critics are noticing, rather, is a typical result of discontinuity of acquaintance: people who meet only in highly specialized capacities aren't usually neighbourly.

3 A person may have roots in a past as well as in a place. He may be rooted to the settlement he inhabits but also to its history. While a person's round of life being localized just involves its being confined to a narrow place, its being rooted involves the sense that he is tied to that place. He identifies with it, feels it to be home and familiar ground. It enters deeply into his sense of who he is. Being rooted in the settlement's history brings a comparable relationship with the past, the sense that the significant events in the history of the settlement are indeed part of one's own life. Having roots, a person perceives his settlement as a persistent object continuous with himself. By identifying with it, the reach of his own life stretches to the physical limits of that larger object and into the past to the events tradition associates with its founding.

A rootless person has no comparable feeling of continuity with a settlement and its past. He may well be single-minded, intensely purposive. He may even identify closely with some larger cause. His rootlessness means only that the identification and sense of continuity with affairs outside himself do not establish an affective relationship with a settlement. He senses no tie to a collective life carried out in a specific locale.

Continuity of acquaintance is simply an overt fact with no implications for people's attitudes or values. But if the people who frequently meet in diverse capacities all have roots in the settlement where they spend their days, a bond by which they sense the significant oneness of their lives is established. In traditional community this sense is tacit, a background not itself brought to sharp consciousness but which nevertheless colours the interpretation of and emotional response to everyday events. A distinctive feature of contemporary cities is that lacking roots the inhabitants' relationships with one another are largely external and not such as to form them into a felt unity.

4 In one sense, our continuity with nature is inescapable. We are subject to gravity, our bodily processes follow the laws of thermodynamics, we age. In thinking of 'nature' we may have in mind these processes. They are natural in that they are beyond our control, although it is possible to influence their impact. In another sense 'nature' refers not to unalterable processes but to objects that have not been transformed by human effort. It scarcely warrants mentioning that in contemporary cities nature in this sense is not much present, while in traditional communities it was pervasive. Ours is largely an environment of man-made objects, and in everyday affairs we have little commerce with natural things. In traditional communities nature was an omnipresent setting. It permeated routine transactions to such an extent that the conception of it as something distinct from rather than an integral dimension of the settlement itself would have been difficult to understand.

Felt continuity with nature consists in this experience of the natural surroundings not being wholly 'other' and apart from oneself and one's community, of the community and the setting forming an integral whole. Tacit identification of oneself with the settlement establishes a distinctive relationship with the natural features of the place as well as with the other inhabitants, living and dead. The streams, hills, and woods that surround the community are familiar. They are not perceived simply as things to be used for the satisfaction of human wants or needs. Although the wood must be cut and the streams fished, use of the natural surroundings is qualified by a conservatism that results from perception of their continuity with the settlement and oneself. The idea of making them over into utilities or commodities does not so readily and persistently arise as it does with urban man. Instead, there is a measure of passivity in the inhabitant's relationship with these natural features. He is disposed to accommodate himself and his wants to them – walk a bit farther to skirt a swamp rather than drain it or build a bridge; follow the shade across the hot courthouse square rather than put up a sun screen. When life is felt as discontinuous with nature, not only is it largely carried out in a setting of man-made objects but people are preoccupied with making over the natural things that surround them to suit their own needs.

5 Finally, life in traditional communities has a predominantly public focus. The centre of gravity, the dimension in which above all else its intrinsic meanings are found, rests firmly in the public domain. Any round of life is discriminable into instrumental activities and those that are final and give point to the whole. Instrumental activities may well become something more than mere means, uninteresting if not painful but necessary nevertheless. But this conversion of an instrumental activity into a positively attractive one depends on there being other activities that have their point or significance in themselves, and that the former are seen to make possible.

Further, some of the activities that form a person's round of life are largely self-maintaining or calculated to satisfy a small enclave with which he is associated, such as the family. Other activities may best be seen as contributing to the quality of life in the settlement as a whole. This contribution is made either indirectly through the consequences of one's actions or directly through the actions themselves. Production of the material conditions of life is an example of the first. Ballet, music, and theatre are examples of the second. The same action may of course form a benefit of both sorts – be beneficial in itself and in its effects.

A person's lifestyle is public in so far as he locates its principal point in activities he sees as contributing to the quality of life of the settlement as a whole. Privatization means using the public domain for private benefits. What matters is the relative weight a person assigns to the public and private spheres, whether he associates the primary meanings with the former or the latter. Privatization is exemplified in the movement of middle-class families to the suburbs, establishing a home there that serves as an oasis within which the point of the round of life is fixed. The city proper then becomes a work place and shopping place; the means of consuming are gained there, and squirrelled back to the enclave out of town.

The public character of life in traditional communities is not so much a consciously held orientation as a background feeling. Moreover, it is a matter of degree and emphasis. Villagers of the past were not wholly preoccupied with the village as a whole as opposed to their own private lives. They were mainly engaged in satisfying quite basic needs. But this effort did not so thoroughly reduce the public sphere to the status of a means: the needs were satisfied through a way of life that was largely public.

III

It is unfortunate that the terms needed to mark the shift from traditional community to contemporary, individualistic patterns of settlement are so charged with honorific and derogatory connotations. 'Continuity' suggests a more admirable condition than 'discontinuity.' Having 'roots' seems preferable to being 'rootless'; being 'publicly' oriented to being 'privatized.' 'Diffuse' is seldom a term of praise. And it is difficult to avoid the assumption that anything that can be called a 'community' must be on balance good.

If we ignore the honorific connotations, however, we will be in a better position to notice the tension between the first trait, localization, and the other four. Being fixed to a specific locale, traditional community exudes confinement and closure. Since the inhabitants are thoroughly settled in a particular place of rather limited extent and self-contained, a sharp boundary divides the settlement from everything outside. All of the objections urbanists make to proposals for restoring community focus on this feature. The small-mindedness and narrowness of villagers, lack of diversified opportunities for self-expression in small places, everyone knowing too much about everyone else with resultant pressures for conformity – these charges get their plausibility from the smallness and inwardness of the places they are directed against.

The other four traits involve transcendence. Under their influence a person lives outside himself. Continuity of acquaintance gives the basis for sensed oneness with the larger group with which his affairs and concerns are intermingled. Continuity with nature means that the whole with which he senses this oneness includes natural features as well as other human beings and man-made things. Being rooted to the settlement means that he catches up in his sense of what he is, not merely the settlement spread out before him but also its past, and in this way he transcends the limits of his own skin and participates in a life that engulfs his own. And the passive orientation that these traits suggest receives an active thrust from the public character of his own lifestyle, by which the objective domain in which he is settled and with which he senses continuity is grasped as also the point and significance of his life.

On the one hand, then, the person in a traditional community transcends his own organic existence by identifying with realities beyond himself. As a result, his life is profoundly outward. His identification with the settlement is natural, not something achieved through deliberation and choice, but a routine outcome of maturing within the settlement's institutions. On the other hand, this transcendence is defeated by the confinement and inwardness of the settlement with which the person identifies. It is not merely that as a result of having identified with a confined place the outwardness of his life is circumscribed to the settlement's limits. But also his mind and outlook mirror the closed character of the place. Since it is self-contained and turned away from the world, his identification with it brings similar inwardness to him.

Dissolution of community leads to loss of the person's natural identification with the setting of his life. By becoming privatized, he loses the pronounced feature of self-transcendence characteristic of life in traditional communities. But the accompanying shift from localized to diffused lifestyles means that people aren't so totally fixed to a particular place. Thus urbanized lifestyles exhibit a tension that parallels that found in traditional communities. No longer fixed to a place a person's horizons are broad. Advanced modes of transportation and communication offer the possibility of ranging widely in space and time. But this openness stands in marked contrast to the self-directed character of the liberated individual's life pursuits. Freed from the closed community he turns inward in self-absorption and private concerns, treating the public domain to which he has more or less unconstrained access not as of intrinsic significance but as a storehouse from which to draw the means for achieving his own satisfactions and comfort.

The plausible objections to restoring traditional communities focus on the stultifying effects of their inwardness and confinement. What one finds admirable in these communities is not this feature but the forms of self-transcendence exhibited in the lives of the inhabitants, in virtue of which they enjoy a stable, if tacit, identification with a larger whole. Urban lifestyles lose this virtue by being privatized, but gain the benefits of individual self-development that result from freeing people from confinement to narrow, largely undifferentiated social environments.

IV

It would seem that the values appealed to by both parties to the dispute about loss of community are reconcilable only by giving up the ideal of spatial community - whether based in villages, small towns, or neighbourhoods - and concentrating instead on functionally defined groups. When a person's principal identifications are with such groups, he is in a position to avoid both the confinement of spatial community and the privatization of a life that doesn't connect with larger social purposes. It may seem in fact that this has already occurred. Urbanists often counter proposals for restoring community to cities through such schemes as the neighbourhood unit plan by arguing that owing to specialization of social functions people's daily rounds take them from one functionally defined group to another, with little continuity of acquaintance between them. The experiences of greatest significance occur in these groups, not in the neighbourhood, whose inhabitants have little in common and no inclination to cross the line that separates familiarity from civility.

The most important groups in this connection are those associated with the various occupations, since specialization is mainly a change in the character of occupations. In terms of day-to-day living, what replaces traditional community for most people are activities and human relationships in the context of a specialized occupation. Specialization involves removal of those activities and relationships from the traditional base of community in neighbourhoods and villages, and loss of community largely refers to the resulting vacuum in that traditional base. Thus, the urbanists' suggestion concerning the role of functionally defined groups may be seen as the proposal that people be helped to find in their occupation, and in the human relationships this involves, the latter-day form of the values that once were sustained by traditional community. But this doesn't so much solve the problem of community as give it a new form. The potential advantage of focusing on an occupation is that through his involvement with it a person may experience self-transcendence. He may find its purposes and way of life to be valuable per se, so that through his participation in it he enjoys a meaningful relationship with the world he inhabits. To realize this advantage, however, two conditions must be satisfied: (1) the occupation must not itself be inward, self-referring, but must be defined by a function that is valuable; (2) and the people associated with it must find the principal reason for their participation to lie in the value they attribute to the activity itself, not in what they get out of it – that is, it must not be privatized.

Of course these conditions may not be satisfied. Often, what a person does in the plant, office, or laboratory is not sensed to be itself worth doing, or worth doing in the light of the social purpose it serves, but is a job he performs in order to earn a living. And the social function may well be valuable only in a restricted way. If the activity produces a commodity, some value is suggested by the fact that people buy it – no doubt people often need what they buy. But the other side of an activity that produces a commodity is that it produces a profit, and it is not cynicism but realism to recognize that pursuit of profit often takes one up different paths than does the attempt to create an admirable object.

The point here is not to condemn people for their motives, or to plead for a change of heart. If the conditions mentioned are seldom satisfied, our attention should be directed not to fancied failings of people to take a moral point of view but to the social definition of occupations.

In our society the closest approximations to occupations that satisfy the two conditions are the professions, in so far as they have retained the character of professions and have not been captured by corporations or become business-oriented. The original 'profession' was a career in the church, and perhaps this first use of the term is responsible for its connotation of being an occupation that is not guided by a self-serving motive but is a form of *service*.

With this connotation in mind, we may say that the direction in which to seek a response to the problem posed by dissolution of community is that suggested by the idea of professionalizing life.

Three features of a profession are relevant in this connection. First, and most basically, each profession is defined by a distinctive social function it performs. Ideally, the benefit created is not exclusive, not directed toward some individuals or groups while working against the interests of others. Particular professions often fail to exemplify this feature. Although in the legal profession defending a client ought to be a way of assuring that justice is done, often in fact the larger purpose drops from sight. And in medicine for years it has seemed that the American Medical Association is a special interest group rather than an organization devoted to supporting the profession's primary function. But developments such as these, though pervasive, are but signs of loss of professional status, of a profession having been converted into a business.

Second, each profession incorporates a distinctive competence, acquired through prior training, by which the characterizing social function is carried out. As a result, the professional is inevitably a specialist.

This is to say that the professional is the one who knows, in the sense of 'knowing-how' – not that his competence and professional life are necessarily narrower than they would be if his occupation were not professionalized. The significant contrast is between a specialist and, say, a dilettante or amateur, one who knows (or ought to) and one who doesn't know (and doesn't pretend to). The latter's activity may indeed be much narrower than the former's; he doesn't thereby become more nearly a specialist or a professional. Thus, it is a mistake to associate being a professional (a 'specialist') with having a narrow occupation (highly specialized), although admittedly many professionalized occupations have split up into numerous, narrow specialties so that often even members of the same profession experience difficulty communicating with one another. It isn't the fact that they are professionalized that is responsible for their high degree of specialization. No doubt there are numerous causes. At the top of the list I would put those forces that currently foster growing bureaucratization of organizations and those responsible for preoccupation with technique, to the point even of converting techniques into ends. Because being a specialist is a central feature of having a profession, we may associate with each profession a distinctive *craft*, and the professional is first of all a *craftsman*.

The social benefit accomplished by the profession may consist simply in expression of this competence itself, as well as in the results of its expression. Thus, we think of the benefits of the medical profession as consisting in the results of applying medical skills, but a musician may be a professional too. A musical performance may well be of benefit to those who hear and appreciate it, of course, but apart from these possibly good consequences of well-played music there is intrinsic value in the performance itself. And there seems no reason for not extending this to all professional performances. A good lecture, a well-argued legal case, a skilful operation are all good in themselves, admirable events in the history of the world. Apart from their effects they immediately enhance the quality of the whole.

Third, with each profession there is associated a written or unwritten code or set of standards that ground a distinction between professional and unprofessional behaviour and that form the profession's charter. In the teaching profession this is largely tacit. In medicine we may think of the Hippocratic Oath. And professional associations often formalize their charter in explicit declarations. One effect of the code is to establish the profession as a moral agency, in the sense of objectifying the understanding that it is part of the conception of the profession that it does not exist to defend some interests against others, but that it contemplates a social contribution that is beneficial from the widest point of view.

Members of a profession often identify with it. They get their sense of what they are in large measure from the social function their professional competence fits them for, construe their profession's charter as a personal code, and gain dignity from assurance that by conscientiously practising a skill that is beneficial in an open-ended way their life has a finally significant point, despite their own individual setbacks, suffering, and finitude. And many people too, not members of recognized professions, reasonably construe their role in the world in the same terms: bring to bear a distinctive competence on a task seen as valuable, however prosaic, and comprehend themselves mainly with reference to this manner of relating with the larger whole on which their activity impinges.

The defect of a traditional community lies in its localization, hence its inwardness, not in the natural identification with their setting that marks the lifestyle of the inhabitants. The idealized 'professional' corrects this defect while continuing to identify himself with a larger whole. Now, however, the identification is not natural but achieved, its seeds sown during the period when the professional competence is acquired. And the unity that results when a number of people with a special competence for carrying out an admirable function identify with that function can scarcely be called a 'community,' since in any case our conception of a complete life must include a diversity of concerns and activities that are only peripheral to any specialized professional pursuit.

V

Ecologists, impressed by the ways we endanger the self-maintaining character of ecosystems in our environment, and by the need to evolve a social system founded on an economy of stock rather than flow – stability rather than growth – are often tempted by the vision of a society articulated into small, self-contained communities in which life has integrity and craftsmanship is a major feature of the daily round. No doubt it is the analogy of such places with the confined ecological communities they know best – in woodlots, lakes, and alpine regions – and the hope of establishing in human communities comparable self-maintaining processes, that is found attractive. Meanwhile, their own lives may exemplify a deep sense of responsibility associated with the widest human concerns, and a highly developed competence devoted to comprehending and acting on those concerns. The social structure they envisage is not one likely to nurture people like themselves, nor is it one they would be likely to find personally satisfying to live within.

If in our model for the future we take as a module not the small community but that relationship with the whole that is found in professional activity at its best, we will be led to a fundamentally different vision, with different implications for urban design and social structure generally. It incorporates the ideals of spatial community and neighbourhood as amenities but is more responsive to the distinctive, individualistic values of urbanized society. Above all, it conceives life as focused on concerns that are more serious and that bestow on the person greater dignity than does the model suggested by ecological analogies.

CHAPTER FOUR

Work and leisure

The lot of most men through the few generations of our existence has been a life of onerous toil, punctuated by brief periods of rest in which to restore energy for the next day's labour. This is a fact that all who long nostalgically for the organic communities of the past should keep well in view, for there is an historical connection between hardship and community. Even in our own day, the occasions for community are principally times of great danger or scarcity. That relationship which was easy and institutionalized in earlier settlements is most closely approximated by us during wartime, when we are brought together against a common enemy; during severe floods or other natural catastrophes, when a common effort is needed to forestall disaster; or during economic depressions, when in their poverty people find that the cheapest available resource is their neighbours.

For some, technology's bright promise is freedom from this life of toil. They envisage a time when, while machines produce the means of life, men at their leisure will pursue projects suggested by their own creative interest, not those dictated by insistent, vital need. In fact, enhanced productivity creates three options, each an alternative to the life of toil. Individually and collectively people have already begun to show their preferences. We may, for example, employ our greatly enhanced capacity to produce by producing more, first to provide all with the means of satisfying vital needs, and then to assure that luxury goods are generally available. In prosaic ways people follow this path when they work overtime or 'moonlight,' or when the husband and wife both work. Nations follow it by adopting an economy of growth: by fixing on the size of the gross national product as a major policy target, by attempting to create jobs and exports, and by encouraging people to consume more.

Or, we may stick to or even lower present consumption levels. Then, by single-mindedly introducing labour-saving devices it would become possible to shrink the labour force drastically. It is no doubt unrealistic to hope that all need for work might be eliminated. But even now our productivity is so great that if growth of population and of new desires were confined, the human prospect could be very substantially transformed from a life of toil to one of leisure. Not many years ago such a suggestion would have seemed fanciful. Today it is commonplace. Many people in their own private lives already have chosen this alternative. Some confine their needs fairly drastically, finding a few weeks of work sufficient to buy a year's leisure. Others, in the affluent corners of the world, have noticed that enough of the affluence falls to the floor as left-overs to eliminate the need to work altogether, provided only that they aren't choosy about what they consume. Whole economies show their preference for leisure by shortening the work day, lengthening vacation periods, and extending the size of the school-going population and increasing the number of years people attend.

Finally, we may take advantage of the fact that enhanced productivity makes efficiency in the narrow sense less necessary. By restructuring the conditions of work, from being toil it might become creative, meaningful activity, humanly significant. The first two options – the consumer-oriented and leisure-oriented societies – require greater efficiency in production. Both concentrate on producing with minimum expenditure of human labour. Work is regarded as a means for gaining other benefits to be enjoyed outside the working period. The third option looks instead to arranging the conditions of work so that it may become intrinsically valuable and interesting, cease to be a means of life but become part of the end for which we live. Individuals choose this alternative by rejecting machine and machine-like production and returning to craftsmanship. Some form agricultural communes in which work is integrated with family life, outmoded farming techniques are followed, and a rather basic standard of living is accepted as a reasonable price to pay for a mode of life in which work is intrinsically satisfying.[1]

These three alternatives aren't mutually exclusive. A person might value luxury consumption along with leisure. And while trying to find more leisure time he might also seek humane working conditions. Nevertheless, they are genuine alternatives. Greater leisure is made possible by increased efficiency in production. But often efficiency is dehumanizing. Making work more humane may make it more inefficient as well, and thus decrease rather than increase the amount of leisure. There are exceptions. If the job is uninteresting there is greater likelihood of absenteeism. Sometimes when it is made more interesting productivity increases. But no one in his right mind who wanted to maximize efficiency would set out simply to make work more deeply satisfying to the workers. When it is found that humanizing the workplace increases efficiency

1 The three models, or their near equivalents, are vividly portrayed in that modern classic by Paul and Percival Goodman, *Communitas* (New York, 1960).

the changes made are essentially cosmetic and the work process is fundamentally directed toward efficiency. A case in point is flexible starting and stopping hours. Some plants have introduced a distinction between core time and flexible time. During core time everyone is on the job. During flexible time, which may be the first two and the last two hours of the working day, a person may arrive or leave when and if he pleases. Often productivity increases when the scheme is adopted, and it certainly makes work more humane. But its success depends on carefully confined application of the principle of flexible time, a confinement that limits the improvement from the workers' point of view. How much more humane it would be to make the entire day flexible time, but how 'unworkable,' that is, inefficient.

Although it is possible to adopt a number of focal values, the three referred to – consumption, leisure, and humanly significant work – tend to defeat one another. We can have luxury consumption and leisure, but to the extent we have either we shall have less of the other. Really to make work humanly significant would be to reduce productivity, lessening the chances for luxury consumption and leisure. Most of us are simply ambivalent. We choose consumption, leisure, and significance in work – but not knowingly or with a sense of the values we are endorsing and those we are compromising. The choices don't so much indicate preference for a multi-focused lifestyle as uncertainty and vacillation regarding fundamental values.

II

The issue may be simplified by dropping the idea of luxury consumption. It is not an option for the future but a passing enthusiasm that can't be sustained. After basic needs have been met, interest in consumption is tied to scarcity – the difficulty of acquiring the goods and the sight of others who aren't so fortunate. Moreover, given anything like the world population we may expect in the near future, luxury consumption for people generally will be impossible. Buckminster Fuller's image of Earth as a space ship has a point he didn't intend. Resources for maintaining the crew are limited and beyond a certain level the by-products of consumption cannot be absorbed.

These facts, that as it becomes widely available luxury consumption doesn't satisfy and that Earth is physically incapable of supporting luxury consumption for people generally, mean that a society that focuses on this value must fail. We saw earlier that the validating experiences implied by a society's focal value must be widely available to those to whom the system intends to distribute them; given the ideal of universalization, this means everyone. And the validating experiences must in fact validate, that is, satisfy. But luxury consumption simply cannot be made generally available, and if it could it wouldn't satisfy.

There remain the options of work and leisure. Shall we direct our efforts toward making work humanly significant, or seek to eliminate it? One of the difficulties in thinking clearly about the issue is the considerable ambiguity of the key terms, work and leisure.

The relevant sense of 'work' when work is opposed to leisure is that of gainful employment. Other senses this leaves out are those intended when we speak of a person's life work, which connotes a career, conceived as issuing in tangible results; work as toil; and that suggested by speaking of a work of art or, more broadly, any activity of making something. A life work is compatible with a life of leisure, and we often make things during leisure time; while toil is too narrow and in any case we cannot seriously inquire into the reasonableness of ordering affairs so that our lives focus on toil.

If we think of work as gainful employment, leisure will be the condition of not being gainfully employed, or the time when a person is in this condition. Fortunately, it isn't necessary to be too precise at this point, since in many contexts the term 'leisure' is exceptionally vague. Thus, we sometimes say of an unemployed person looking for work that he is doing so in his leisure time. But a society of unemployed people would not be called a leisure-*oriented* society. And not everything a person does during the time he is not working is said to be a leisure activity – sleeping, for example, or driving the children to school. A housewife not gainfully employed would resist the description of herself as living a life of unrelieved leisure.

Work has a twofold significance of producing something both for oneself and for society at large. It creates goods and services that have utility for others. But also it is remunerated and thus produces a capability of consuming on the part of the persons who work. When people produced for their own consumption alone – when, as food-gatherers, it was as direct as picking a berry and then swallowing it – these two aspects of work were not separated. If a person owns the object he produces, and it is intended for his own consumption rather than for trade, having the object in hand as a result of expenditure of effort is one side of a fact the other side of which is having a capability of consuming. In such circumstances it would be pedantic to distinguish the two aspects of work. But, as Karl Marx noticed, when directed toward commodity production work is a social process.[2] Its two aspects are institutionally separated. The product is intended for someone else, while the worker's capability of consuming is a result of being paid for his labour. Work becomes a social process in the sense that because the object produced is a commodity, in producing it one enters into relations with others. This occurs regardless of whether the productive activity is co-operative or the person works entirely alone.

2 *Capital*, ed. F. Engels (London, 1887), I, pp. 41-55.

The character of the social process involved is determined by the society's economic institutions.

A leisure-oriented society is possible because of labour-saving devices, especially automated production processes. Imagine a technology so advanced that no human labour is used in commodity production and all services are performed by machines – a condition that Aristotle alluded to by imagining every tool doing its own work, unguided by slaves.[3] It isn't important that practically speaking this condition, though approachable, is not achievable. What we want to see are the implications of approximating it. By eliminating work we would eliminate both the activities by which people produce commodities and also those by which they produce their capability of consuming. On one side, we would have the commodities and on the other a leisured population who, not 'gainfully employed,' could not in the usual way get possession of them. With elimination of wages a new principle of distribution would be needed, some practice for determining a person's share of the available commodities. If there were no scarcity the issue wouldn't arise. But under any reasonable assumption regarding the eventual size of the world's population, the waste products of unlimited consumption would choke us. If the amount of money a person earns by working does not determine his share of the available commodities, what will?

One possibility is simple equality: everyone might be given an equal share regardless of differential needs. Another is expressed in Marx's formula, to each according to his need. It isn't clear how the first part of the formula, from each according to his ability, was intended to interact with this, but in any case it drops out as irrelevant here since with machines doing the work the individual's contribution according to ability is not required. Or Aristotle's principle might be considered: to each according to his contribution to the purpose of the state, the maintenance of a high quality of life.

These alternative principles of distribution sever the tie between a person's capability of consuming and his contribution to commodity production, his work. Since in a leisure society there is no work some such alternative must be found. Whatever it is, the result will not be capitalism as that term is understood in Marxist theory. According to Marx, capitalism is essentially a 'wages system.' The 'free wage labourer' sells his labour power to another – the capitalist – who uses it to produce surplus value. The labourer adds more value to the product than the capitalist pays for use of the labour power. By selling the product the capitalist converts this surplus value into profit. On this analysis, if there is no work there can be no profit, therefore no capitalists.

3 '... as if a shuttle should weave of itself ... ' 1253b. *The Politics of Aristotle*, trans. E. Barker (Oxford, 1946), p. 10.

Even if we reject Marx's claim that profit-making requires exploitation of wage-labourers by extracting surplus labour from them, we may still see some point in thinking of capitalism as essentially a wages system, since this highlights what is important in the transition from feudalism to capitalism. The former was a system in which persons were tied to the soil and legally bound to work for a lord, for which their payment, by which their own capability of consuming was gained, was free time in which to farm strips of land for themselves. The passage from feudalism to capitalism involved freeing people from the land so that they were able to sell their labour power. Capability of consuming then was gained by payment of money rather than free time.

When capitalism is thought of in this way, as a system in which people sell their labour for a price, thereby acquiring a capability of consuming, the leisure society must be seen as post-capitalistic. If we imagine that as a result of technological 'progress,' replacement of working men by machines and electronic devices, such a society is bound to evolve, we must accept that one of Marx's main predictions, that capitalism will develop conditions leading to its overthrow, will prove correct. But such a post-capitalist society could very well include autonomous corporations which largely dispense with human labour but nevertheless realize a profit on sale of their product. In this case, another of Marx's main predictions would prove dramatically incorrect. For such a system would probably evolve not through a confrontation between the proletariat and capitalist classes but through the initiative of the corporations themselves. Enlightened conservatives are beginning to see the business advantages of a guaranteed annual wage, which is in a limited way an alternative to the wages system and doesn't guarantee 'wages' but provides an income floor, and it is an historic policy of organized labour to resist labour-saving devices.

III

The larger significance of the idea of a leisure-oriented society is the change in human relationships brought by focusing life on leisure activities. We understand leisure as time in which people are primarily satisfying themselves, pursuing their own interests or enthusiasms. The activity they take up may have social value. But what makes it leisure is that it is not taken up as being necessary. Being free time, how a person uses it is his own affair. It would be wrong to stress this self-referring aspect to the point of suggesting that if activity produces a benefit for others it is not leisure. And of course in his leisure time a person may be motivated by a sense of duty. But in the main our idea of a leisure-oriented society does not envisage people engaged in benefitting others or motivated by a sense of duty. Rather, we think of people as being largely freed from dependence on one another, so that there are few occasions for acting from a sense of duty, and no great need to be engaged in producing benefits for others. In the leisure society a person serves himself not because he lacks conscientiousness but because human affairs have reached such a stage that it is possible conscientiously to turn his attention to his own destiny.

The self-referring character of the leisure-oriented society results from the fact that a world of work is one in which people depend on one another for the satisfaction of basic needs. As a rule, people don't work in order to produce commodities needed by others, but do so rather for the sake of what they get out of it, a capability of consuming. Still, the social aspect is there, regardless of whether anyone is motivated by it. To eliminate work is to eliminate the principal sources of our dependence on one another. And though a person would then become dependent on the machines that do the work, he would no longer be depended upon and so might turn to self-referring pursuits. Indeed in many respects he would have no alternative to doing so. To reject the leisure-oriented society and accept the inefficiency consequent to humanizing work is to reject the possibility of freeing people from dependence on one another.

Basic values are at stake in the choice between a leisure-oriented and work-oriented society. When work is humanly significant it not only satisfies the worker but unlike much contemporary work produces objects that satisfy the genuine needs of others. The work-oriented society finds its primary values in activities by which the conditions for social and individual life are produced. The leisure-oriented society delegates these activities to machines and locates value instead in activities that are adopted as spontaneous expressions of a person's creativity or conditions of his self-development. Shall we use our greatly enhanced productivity to free each from the rest, except for those dependencies implied by love, intimacy, and friendship, which are intelligible only if they arise spontaneously from the personal needs and interests of the persons who express them? Or shall we bring more generous standards than narrow efficiency to the activities by which the conditions of individual and collective life are produced, so that those activities may become more humane and have a more humane result?

IV

The focal value of the leisure-oriented society is simply freedom, in the sense of permissiveness. Fully stated, the ideal is that people will confront an environment so open that their days and nights are taken up with activities that reflect uncoerced choices of their own. Lacking structure, the setting permits everything and demands nothing. Obviously this is an ideal in the sense of a limit, an unreachable but indefinitely approachable condition. We can realistically contemplate opening up the field for individual decision without limit, but not actually achieving a condition where that field is in fact unlimited.

The validating experiences of a society ordered around freedom as a focal value are those associated with creative activity and intimacy: first, meeting a challenge to create an object that gives satisfying form to some impulse; second, close personal communication with others. These may of course occur together. Creativity and intimacy appear to be the pre-eminent modes of deeply satisfying self-expression. Their effect of validating the social system in which they occur depends on their being utterly uncoerced and spontaneous, and on its being evident that they are not wedged into the interstices of the system but are a predictable and intended outcome of its design.

Against the background of this account of the leisure-oriented society's focal value and validating experiences, its idealized character types or heroes come into view. The heroes will be people whose personal virtues complement the focal value by bestowing marked competence for having and appreciating the validating experiences. Such virtues are openness, uninhibitedness, and lack of rigidity, traits that ground capacities for giving the stamp of oneself to objects and for intimacy with others. With these capacities the formally open, permissive environment may become a domain in which options are spontaneously taken up and people's awareness of an assured power to grow lends a pervasive buoyancy to the scene. The prevalent 'moral point of view' will primarily consist of distaste for the very idea of a moral point of view. Moral rules as guides in life will be rejected as signs of personal closure and rigidity. Actions will be judged not so much by objective, formal standards as by the degree of vitality expressed and growth achieved.

What sorts of institutions would we evolve if we unambiguously chose the leisure-oriented society as our model for the future? We would find the anti-technology response to environmental issues excessively defensive. We would willingly take up innovations made possible by advanced technology in so far as doing so did not threaten the underlying conditions of our existence. Not wishing to return to nature, neither would we wish to confine our horizons to the narrow limits of old-style intentional communities or latter-day adaptations. A negative attitude toward technology would undercut the practices that make leisure possible, while in intentional community the tie of person with group implies a structure and discipline at odds with the goal of an open, permissive setting in which uncoerced choice occurs. Rather, the social structure would avoid bureaucratic patterns of organization, and institutions would be conceived as arrangements for facilitating fulfilment of people's spontaneously arising purposes while not channelling activity in predetermined directions. Institutions would be in effect collections of tools for accomplishing quite broadly defined ends, and would incorporate mechanisms for reorientation as impulses to grow and express oneself in new directions appeared. Architecture and urban design would not so much seek to arrange spaces specifically tailored for doing antecedently decided upon things – regardless of how 'client' or 'user' oriented the designer was – but would design flexible, adaptable spaces, incorporating an aesthetic that calls attention to the flexibility.

The competing model of a work-oriented society envisages work and interdependence, but the work is satisfying and produces objects that are not frivolous. With us, work is a means to ends that fall outside the work sphere. In a work-oriented society work is the central feature of the total way of life, integral with the rest. Organicity and the integrity of the way of life are dominant themes. For work to become the activity that above all lends significance to individual life, it must both be humanized and produce socially valuable objects. Production processes would need to be decentralized and organized around work teams that co-operatively see through complex tasks and within which *esprit* and a sense of identification might develop. Tasks at work would be set up so as to require judgment, and this not just at the highest levels of management but at all the points where the actual work is occurring, where hands are touching tools. Work would once again become risky: but the possibility of failure brings also human responsibility for success.

'Technique' means elimination of this possibility and responsibility. Automation is the apotheosis of technique, and the effect generally of bringing advanced technology to bear on production processes is to introduce techniques that eliminate judgment and (it is hoped) reduce risk. Paradoxically, then, the project of humanizing work is at odds with that of humanizing technology. The latter contemplates improving the results of our applications of technology so that those affected may find their lives enhanced not strangled. The technology of steel production, for example, is humanized by incorporating processes in which water used in the production is purified before being drained away. These processes may involve quite advanced 'techniques' that exclude human judgment and responsibility for the result and that are in fact dehumanizing from the worker's point of view. In light of the association of technology with perfection of 'technique' in this sense, the work-oriented society would be fundamentally opposed to advanced technology. The objection would not be that often voiced by organized labour, that technology tends to replace men by machines, but that it routinizes tasks and thus uses men as we do machines.

The opposite of technique is craftsmanship. We may think of the craftsman as one whose manner of making something involves a high risk of failure, for the avoidance of which his skill and judgment are essential.[4] To use the term

4 The view of technique expressed here, and of its relation with craftsmanship, is suggested by J. Ellul, *The Technological Society*, trans. J. Wilkinson (New York, 1964), chap. 1. But it is more explicitly developed out of a critique of Ruskin by D. Pye, *The Nature and Art of Workmanship* (Cambridge, 1968).

this way is to dissociate craftsmanship and handicraft, working with one's hands rather than with machines. A person who works up material with his hands, making use of no tools at all, might do so in a highly routinized way, without adapting his activity to individual characteristics of the material at hand and without attempting to individualize the objects he makes. Another person may operate complex machinery sensitively and flexibly, so that not merely his skill but his character shows in the result. We want a definition of craftsmanship that identifies the latter as the better craftsman despite his greater reliance on machinery. What distinguishes his activity is that the quality of the product requires unerring judgment and skill. If these fail the product will suffer accordingly; the production process is not ordered so as to squeeze out their influence.

Just as it is irrelevant to craftsmanship whether the craftsman works with his hands or with machines, so it is irrelevant to having a technology whether machines are used in the production process or whether the technology is labour-intensive. The Egyptians had a sophisticated technology for pyramid construction but it was labour-intensive. The sophistication consisted in successful routinization of tasks. Identification of technological sophistication with use of complicated machinery and electronic devices is a natural mistake, since so far as a production process is routinized men participate in a machine-like way. But this means only that the association of technology with machinery is metaphorical.

The work-oriented society will be craft-oriented, but not artsy-craftsy and not in a sense that involves working with one's hands rather than with power-driven tools. It will be craft-oriented in that the worker's skills and judgment will be depended on, so that there is risk of failure and he is responsible for the result.

Finally, a work-oriented society, in which work is a central element in an integral way of life, will value community. If work is to be an integral element in the way of life, and we are to have decentralization, then the natural units of social organization will be small communities. We may think of a self-contained neighbourhood, through which small work shops are interspersed, and of a flow of life that knows no abrupt changes of pace and discontinuities as there is passage from family life or shopping or socializing to working. No particular period of time would be specifically and rigidly devoted to work and work places would not be used solely for that purpose.

The focal value of a work-oriented society would be the way of life itself. The principal meanings would be experienced in work, by which a valuable and valued contribution to the community is made. Validating experiences would be those associated with work: first, the sense of working constructively in co-operation with others on a serious project of value to the entire community – one thinks of a group of Chinese enjoying their comradeship working together on a road-building project under a summer sun; second, the satisfaction a craftsman might feel, employing his skill and judgment in creating an object he knows will be put to a good use. The contrasts with the validating experiences of a leisure-oriented society should be noted - of co-operation in work with intimacy between friends, and of disciplined craftsmanship that creates an object of use to others with free self-expression.

The distinctive idealized character traits of the work-oriented society would be discipline, devotion, seriousness. The centre of gravity in a person's life would be outside himself, in his work, and in the local group who share his way of life. It would be a mistake to overstress the contrasts. There is room for fun and playfulness in a life focused on work, and for gravity in self-directed pursuits. In any case, one wants balance and to avoid onesidedness. But the central theme of the society, its *focal* value, sets the dominant tone.

V

Both models are highly attractive. We are bound to value the key themes of a leisure-oriented society - individuality and arrangements that nurture freedom and spontaneity. Equally, we must respect a communal way of life in which there is work to be done and where through work a person finds his place in and value for the community. Some lean toward one of the models, some toward the other. Some sense excessive dependence of the individual on the group in a work-oriented society. Others are disturbed by the permissiveness and lack of structure of a leisure-oriented society, and sense greater seriousness in a communal, work-orientation. But none can deny that both models merit respect and are not to be dismissed out of hand.

The very attractiveness of each, however, is the source of our inability wholly to endorse the other, for it is essential to each that it excludes just those features on which the other focuses. The work-oriented society excludes leisure except as an incident, and the leisure-oriented society excludes work as far as possible. A person who lives in and is oriented toward a community does not desire a totally open, permissive environment in which he may consult just himself, find and act out what *he* really wants. And one whose enthusiasm is self-expression is directed away from the community with its closure and ties. Each model, owing to its distinctive virtues, forms an effective critique of the other and tends to cancel it.

It may be said that this negative result was made inevitable by the decision to separate out two sides of a good idea, and build around each a model of the future that excludes the other. This would suggest that all we need do is think of a world in which there is work and leisure, each to balance the other, rather than single-mindedly focus on just one. But to respond in this eclectic way would be to avoid the issue rather than take up the challenge it poses. In any case in the foreseeable future there will be plenty of work and plenty of leisure. But to incorporate both in our model of the sort of world we would like to see evolve would be to regard as an ideal state of affairs a compromise solution in which the full value of each orientation is sacrificed in the interest of accommodating some of the value of the other. In so doing, we would fail to resolve our own ambivalence concerning quite fundamental values.

The challenge is to integrate the admitted values of a work- and leisure-oriented society, but so that we are left not with a compromise but with a positive ideal. A clue to what this might involve was provided by the idea of professionalism introduced in the last chapter. Professionalization of occupations was seen as a means of overcoming the narrowness of spatial community while avoiding the alienation implied by highly individualistic lifestyles. There, attention was focused on a person's relations with his colleagues when his principal occupation is professionalized. Here, the relevant feature is the immediate impact of professionalism on the person's relation with the occupation itself. A good way to grasp the significance of the fact that an occupation has been professionalized is to contrast this with other means of controlling it. To simplify matters, let us suppose that every occupation is concerned with producing an object or service for a client, by which some need of the client's is catered for. There are occupations that don't have clients, and even when they do the point of the occupation isn't always to satisfy a need. Pure mathematicians don't have clients, for example, except incidentally, and it distorts the profession of a concert pianist to suppose that he plays in order to satisfy his audience's need for music. Nevertheless, the simplification is convenient and should do no harm. Control of an occupation largely involves authority to determine precisely what the client needs and how it will be catered for. There are three possibilities: the client may control these matters, the people who carry on the occupation may, or some third party may intervene on behalf of both the producer and his client. The first of these modes of control of an occupation has been called *patronage*, the second *collegiate*, the third *mediated.*[5] Patronage typically occurs when the people who carry on the occupation are connected with and controlled by a ruling family or corporation. Or, when there are numerous, heterogeneous clients it may take the form of consumerism and be supported by a strong consumers' association. Mediated control might result from extensive governmental intervention in the producer-consumer relationship, as in some forms of socialized medicine, or from interven-

5 These distinctions are borrowed from T. Johnson, *Professions and Power* (London, 1972). Although I lean heavily on Johnson's typology, I am putting it to a use that he would almost certainly reject. Moreover, his discussion is flawed by the assumption that professionals always have 'clients' with 'needs' that are to be 'catered for.'

tion by a capitalist, as in the case of clinics and nursing homes operated for profit. Collegiate control was instanced in the guild system and, more recently, in the rise of professions.

The distinctive feature of professionalism considered as a manner of controlling an occupation is that it involves autonomy. Use of the term 'collegiate' calls attention to the autonomy of the occupation as a whole: the practitioners, as a group of colleagues, control the occupation. But the autonomy must extend in considerable degree to the individual practitioner, a feature that underlies his 'practice.' Without this, each member of the profession is controlled by the profession as a whole, which then would function as an intervening third party between the 'professional' and his client. The autonomy of the individual practitioner involves his control of his practice – of the overall context in which it will be carried on, and of the relationship he enters into with his clients.

If now we give up the assumption that he necessarily has a client with needs that he caters for, we may broaden the idea of a professionalized occupation by saying that it involves a specialized competence for pursuing a distinctive purpose. To professionalize the occupation is to structure it so that those who possess the specialized competence are made responsible for determining how it shall be applied in the relevant sphere of activity. And to carry on the occupation in a professional manner is to accept this responsibility by bringing one's competence to bear on the matter at hand without being diverted by such extraneous purposes as a desire to please an audience or client, or to realize some personal benefit from the activity. The point is not that audiences and clients aren't to be pleased, or that personal benefits aren't to be gained and seen as important. But if the activity is professional these come as a consequence of the activity having succeeded in its own terms, that is, of it satisfying the standards of the profession itself.

In a professionalized occupation, then, autonomy is coupled with outwardness, self-transcendence. The freedom that the advocate of a leisure-oriented society pursues is essential to professionalism as well. But leisure brings freedom in the form of permissiveness. It involves a life that has no point that transcends the leisured person and that does not connect him with the world in a serious way. When a person focuses his life on an occupation that has been professionalized, and carries it on in a professional manner, his freedom is expressed in activity directed toward ends that refer to the world at large beyond himself. He sees these ends as valuable per se, and he sees his life as gaining meaning from the opportunity of contributing to them that his occupation presents.

Professionalism, so defined, is an ideal type. Moreover, the definition is stipulative. The type of occupation stipulated is sufficiently like those we commonly call 'professions' that there are only two sensible alternatives: to coin an altogether new term to refer to the type, or simply to label it 'professionalism' and hope that inappropriate associations can be avoided.[6] Toward this end it is important to keep in mind that the current debate in many occupations over whether or how to 'professionalize' them is not necessarily a debate about professionalism in the sense intended here. And many so-called professions have not as yet become, or have ceased to be, professionalized.

Professionalism forms, then, a plausible alternative to work and leisure, and holds promise of realizing in one coherent focus the values that make both the work-oriented and the leisure-oriented societies attractive. It isn't important whether one regards the alternative as a version of the work-oriented model, on the basis that it locates the centre of gravity in life in one's occupation, or considers it to be a third alternative that while recommending neither a work nor a leisure orientation shares features of both. But since I shall be principally concerned to develop the distinctive features of professionalism, it will be convenient to conceive it in the latter way, as a third alternative.

Nevertheless, it is clear that professionalism has more extensive implications for the structure of work than it has for the structure of leisure. The same antithesis that was found between the models of a work-oriented and a leisure-oriented society is continued when we contrast the model of a society in which work is replaced by professionalization of occupations with the leisure-oriented model. The shift from work to professionalism, however, suggests a complementary shift in our conception of leisure.

The Greeks, less committed to relating all of their fundamental ideas with the sphere of work, had a more promising conception of leisure than that which identifies it with free time, and one that complements professionalism. With them, 'leisure' often had a primarily adverbial use. In this use, to act leisurely is to take a distinctively aesthetic stance. The significance of one's activity is then seen to be intrinsic to it, the present is savoured for its own sake, and one is not busy working for some future result in such a way that the value of present activity is deferred and made dependent on the activity's contribu-

6 In some respects the term 'craft' is more apt than 'profession' for the kind of occupation I am referring to. Unfortunately, 'craft' doesn't have natural verbal, adjectival, and participial forms. What shall we put for 'professionalize,' 'professionalization,' and 'professionalism'? And then 'craft' has its own misleading connotations. Nevertheless, at the core of any 'profession' in the intended sense is a *craft*, a method that can be learned, and the professionals are all of those who have and practise the craft. In 'The Social Significance of Professional Ethics,' in the *Annals of the American Academy*, CI (May 1922), pp. 5-11, R.M. MacIver develops a conception of professionalism that is in most important respects the same as that intended here. At that time it was possible to represent the discussion as an account of *existing* professions. Today that would be naïve.

tion to that result. Aristotle's prime examples were music and philosophical speculation. They needn't be *for* something else. Their value lies in themselves and appreciating them involves being absorbed in and contented with the present – with what one is doing at the time and what one perceives around oneself. The music heard or played, the interchange of ideas, are sensed as *sufficient.* One is attentive but at ease, not looking past the present into the future where, it is imagined, the point of what one is presently about is to be found.[7]

The essential contrast, then, is between being leisurely and busy. It seems likely that our own concept of leisure as free time is a corruption of the Greek idea, resulting from our identifying being busy with working, busyness with business. Where we think of leisure as free time, the Greek concept makes being leisurely a distinctive way of relating with time. Busyness involves forcing the pace. The clock ticks and one is constantly leaning toward the tick coming next. Being leisurely involves placing oneself in the stream of events, allowing its pace and cadence to carry one along. Leisurely action is not devoted to wrenching the stream of events to a new direction that one *wills*, but is fitted to the stream and seeks to complete it, give or continue its wholeness. In *War and Peace* Kutuzov fought a leisurely war, Napoleon a busy one.

The Greeks' distaste for work led them to believe that to be of any interest leisurely activity must be useless. Music and contemplation aren't good *for* very much, and Aristotle saw this as a mark in their favour. Two recent au-

7 In Book X of the *Nicomachean Ethics*, Aristotle relates 'leisure' and contemplation in an instructive way: 'And this [contemplative] activity alone would seem to be loved for its own sake; for nothing arises from it apart from the contemplating, while from practical activities we gain more or less apart from the action. And happiness is thought to depend on leisure; for we are busy that we may have leisure, and make war that we may live in peace ... So if among virtuous actions political and military actions are distinguished by nobility and greatness, and these are unleisurely and aim at an end and are not desirable for their own sake, but the activity of reason, which is contemplative, seems both to be superior in serious worth and to aim at no end beyond itself, and to have its pleasure proper to itself (and this augments the activity), and the self-sufficiency, leisureliness, unweariedness (so far as this is possible for man), and all the other attributes ascribed to the supremely happy man are evidently those connected with this activity, it follows that this will be the complete happiness of man, if it be allowed a complete term of life ... ' 1177^b, 1-24. *Ethica Nicomachea*, trans. W.D. Ross (Oxford, 1925).

And in *Politics*: 'The feelings which play produces in the mind are feelings of relief from exertion; and the pleasure it gives provides relaxation. Leisure is a different matter: we think of it as having in itself intrinsic pleasure, intrinsic happiness, intrinsic felicity. Happiness of that order does not belong to those who are engaged in occupation: it belongs to those who have leisure' 1337^b–1338^a. *The Politics of Aristotle*, trans. E. Barker (Oxford, 1946), p. 336.

It must be acknowledged, however, that there is no one 'Greek sense of the term "leisure" ' and that even Aristotle uses the term in more than one way.

thors who have attempted to resuscitate the Greek conception of leisure, J. Pieper and S. De Grazia, have made the mistake of building Greek feelings about work into their definitions.[8] They assert that if an activity is good for anything it simply isn't leisure. But this is clearly a mistake. Digging a ditch may be just as leisurely an occupation as listening to the lyre. The fact that later on water may run into the ditch, thus draining a field so that crops might grow, is beside the point. What makes it leisurely is not its being good for nothing beyond itself, but how it is done. The digger may in fact be passionately interested in the good his digging does, just as the general wanted very much to win the war. He digs leisurely by not forcing the pace, valuing the activity itself, matching action to reaction in which the pleasurable sensations of doing a job well are savoured. Although the work produces a benefit that will be enjoyed later, everything isn't sacrificed to that future benefit.

It is, I suppose, true that many people fail to lead leisurely lives because they are too busy making money, or perhaps busy working without earning much money. If such people would or could devote more time to pursuits that are useless they might also begin to live in a more leisurely fashion. But there is no guarantee, and it is at least possible that they would find leisure more readily in activity that is of great use both to themselves and to others.

Professional activity not only may be leisurely but in the best circumstances will be. Distinctively professional activity expresses a specialized competence that uniquely fits the person for performing a characteristic task. Assured possession of the competence is shown in activity that has a leisurely pace. It neither drags nor is rushed but moves at the rate the unfolding events themselves require. In the surgery, football stadium, or concert hall, a mark of professional competence is economy of movement. By not forcing events, the person who has the competence does not put himself in the position of willing the result he seeks, of imposing it. Rather he co-operates with a process already underway and perceived as independent of himself, making a contribution that may induce the process to yield up the desired result.

A consequence is that professional activity exhibits a measure of impersonality. This is not to say that the professional is uninterested in the outcome. But so far as he is confident he realizes that he has done what was appropriate so that failure to achieve the result sought means only that practically speaking success was not in the cards. Impersonality means that there is distance between oneself and the particular problem to which the activity is addressed. When the physician who has lost his patient or the lawyer his case is quite sure of the adequacy of the professional skills he brought to bear his regret at the

8 Pieper, *Leisure, the Basis of Culture*, trans. A. Dru (New York, 1963); De Grazia, *Of Time, Work & Leisure* (New York, 1962).

outcome does not manifest itself as self-recrimination. Rather, the response has a universal character, in which are combined awareness of fate and of the limited powers of humans to influence events. Of course confidence in one's skills can be carried so far as to be either unbelievable or inhuman. But this is only to admit that we do not admire the pretense of total professionalism.

Impersonality and distance are similarly present in all leisurely activity. This shows in the attitude of acceptance it involves. The leisurely person dwells in the present and allows himself to be carried along. As the events succeed one another no particular one is grasped and held fast and the outcome toward which they move is not sweatingly anticipated.

A further suggestion of the relationship of professionalism and leisureliness is found in the fact that we commonly refer to a completed professional activity as a 'performance.' The activity is thus identified as of value in itself, apart from its results, a connected sequence of movements that together form a significant whole, 'the performance.' By referring to the activity in this way we attribute to it the characteristics which, when appreciated by the professional 'actor' himself, make it leisurely.

When leisure is conceived as free time it is opposed to work. A society that adopts one as its focal value to that extent denies the other. In saying this I am not taking advantage of what may be regarded as arbitrary definitions of work and leisure that tie the first to activity for which a person is paid and the second to activity for which he is not paid. At a deeper level there is the fact that leisure as free time suggests time when one is freed from the dependence of others, while work as a social practice presupposes such dependence. Professionalism and leisure in the Greek sense, by contrast, support one another. A society that pursues both will have a coherent focus, and its success in each pursuit will enhance the chances of success in the other. Such a society implies different institutions and will be guided by a different aesthetic and different principles of urban design than will one that adopts either a work orientation or a leisure orientation as its model.

VI

The model of a work-oriented society is formed by responses to the issues discussed in this and the preceding two chapters. The three aims it incorporates are withdrawal of commitment to technology, rebuilding community, and humanizing work. From the other side, the three aims of the leisure-oriented society are humanizing the impact of technology, perfecting individualized lifestyles characteristic of urbanized areas, and maximizing leisure time. These are the elements of the principal models of the future that our intellectual tradition suggests. Discussion of the issues has, however, introduced three leading ideas that are either not stressed or are positively rejected by both models: responsibility, professionalism, and leisure in the Greek sense of the term.[9]

Before developing these ideas to see what kind of alternative model they suggest, I want to consider the work- and leisure-oriented models from two further points of view. Each reflects a fairly general world-view in terms of which people order their individual lives and their perception of the world, ground their hopes for the future or their despair, and comprehend their past. One of these world-views may be referred to as wholism, the other as individualism. Just as some people tend to be extraverted and some introverted, some active and some passive, so also some seem congenitally wholistic in outlook, some individualistic. These are background habits of thought that direct our enthusiasms and aversions, not necessarily consciously held ideas. A wholistic world-view prompts a person to opt for the three responses that constitute the work-oriented model with the same inevitability and conviction that his opposite number, whose outlook is basically individualistic, shows in opting for the responses that constitute the leisure-oriented model.

These world-views manifest themselves in two ways. They find conceptual expression in philosophical systems. But also they shape the kinds of settlement people build. In the first case, the tension between them is reflected in an argument between individualistic and wholistic philosophers. In the second case, it is reflected in the competition between town culture and village culture. The town, to use one term to cover the full range of settlements from market towns to megalopolises, is, in view of fundamental features of the lifestyles it settles, the historic embodiment and objectification of individualism. The village, a smaller, more insular, and self-contained form of settlement, is the historic home and expression of wholism. In Chapter 6 I shall review the conceptual expression of the two world-views in the philosophies of Hegel and John Stuart Mill. But first, in Chapter 5, two main features of the contrast between town and village culture will be considered.

9 It will be noted that I have introduced two contrasting ideas that are referred to by use of the same term, 'leisure.' Whenever the model of a leisure-oriented society is mentioned, leisure in the sense of free time is intended. Similarly, 'leisure time' throughout means free time. All adverbial uses of leisure are to be understood in the other, Greek, sense of absorption in the present. The context should forestall ambiguity. I have rejected the alternative of avoiding terminological confusion by adopting some such term as 'ludic behaviour' to refer to being leisurely, since this and the others that come to mind are either inaccurate or graceless.

CHAPTER FIVE

Town and village

After perhaps two million years as a food-gatherer and hunter, some eleven thousand years ago man invented agriculture. In itself the invention was of no great significance, since primitive farming was not startlingly different from the late stages of food-gathering. It is only with an eye to what followed that we may say that it represented an advance, or even a notable invention. Sometime earlier, in Europe, for example, men lived off reindeer: they understood their ways and no doubt in many respects controlled their behaviour, and systematically culled the herds that they spent their lives following. We do not call this animal husbandry; and yet the art and knowledge involved probably exceeded that required of the first peasants who raised their own goats, and it may have provided a more adequate and secure food supply.

The most momentous result of the invention of agriculture was that it permitted and required settled life. Previously, and for more than 99 per cent of his existence on the planet, man *camped* but did not routinely settle. He bedded down near the current food supply and moved on when it had been used up. The original food-growers were fixed to a place by their manner of acquiring food. The longer they stayed in the same place the more suitable it became for their purposes, while among food-gatherers the reverse was usually the case. There is nothing particularly momentous about a shift from moving around a great deal to spending one's entire life in the same place. But staying in the same place, and settling into it, involved creating a human environment. Previously, human life was spent in a natural domain to which men adapted. They plundered, but did not make it over. They were usually the dominant living species within the domain they inhabited, but that domain did not form a distinctively human world. Settling in brought physical and psychological changes. Fields were cleared, land cultivated, dwellings and places of worship built. And a human mentality emerged that was adapted to the new setting of human life and to the lifestyle it involved. Initially, these human environments formed pockets of settlement within a largely natural world, little human worlds within *the* world. During the more than ten thousand years since settled life began, however, these pockets of settlement have spread so that now the emphasis is reversed. We think of the natural domain as existing beyond a vanishing frontier, beyond the boundaries of *the*, that is, the human, world, and see nature as something to be preserved from further encroachment or as a source of scarce raw material to be allocated wisely.

Almost from the beginning settled life took two forms that existed side by side, villages and towns. The picture many have is of an indefinitely long period of life in peasant communities, followed at the end of the Late Chalcolithic, around 3500 B.C., by the emergence of urban civilizations in Egypt and Mesopotamia. But what one takes to be recent or contemporaneous depends on the time scale one refers the events to. The important fact is that man lived approximately two million years before he began routinely to inhabit settlements. Settled life cannot have become the normal human condition before, say, 10,000 B.C. And in at least two settlements, Jericho and Çatal Hüyük, which existed over nine thousand years ago, life was so advanced and complex that it would be highly misleading to call them villages. At the most, then, only three thousand years elapsed between emergence of the first peasant communities and the first full-fledged towns, and it is probable that the spread was somewhat less than that. In relation to the length of time preceding the beginnings of settled life, and the duration of the succeeding period, in which both forms of settlement have been prevalent, we cannot suppose the time span between the first peasant communities and the first full-fledged towns to have been long. And it is arguable that town life preceded *secure* peasant communities and made them possible. It seems reasonable then to hold that both arose during the same era, as contrasting responses to the possibility and need for settlement created by the invention of agriculture.

In archaeological terms, this era is conventionally designated as Proto-Neolithic, roughly dated, for the Near East, between 9000 and 7000 B.C. Of this era the discoverer of Çatal Hüyük has written:

Even without actual grain, the presence of numerous querns and mortars, pounders and grinders – which now appear for the first time [in Jordan, Iran, and Anatolia]; the storage pits and the sickle blades all tell the same story of a change in the economy. At the same time we find the first traces of permanent settlements, frequently rebuilt. Cemeteries appear and the graves contain luxury objects such as beads and pendants, which show that man had leisure and time for other things than appeasing his hunger. Art makes its appearance in the form of animal carvings and statuettes of the supreme deity, the Mother

Goddess. Trade increases and by the end of the period the first towns are built, already girt with a defensive wall often of massive proportions.[1]

In this chapter I want to consider the differences between town culture and village culture. Obviously towns are larger places than villages. But there are important differences in their lifestyles as well, and it is these that give content to the claim that the model of a work-oriented society contemplates in effect the perfection of village life, while that of a leisure-oriented society contemplates the perfection of town life.

As will be seen, the distinctive feature of village culture is its self-sufficiency. This involves insularity in the sense of independence of the outside world and in the sense that the inhabitants have minimal contact with outsiders. And it also involves establishment within the village of a common way of life that the inhabitants apprehend as the focal point of their individual existences. Town life, by contrast, is open in that there is extensive interdependence with life outside and in that the townsman's way of life brings him into frequent contact with outsiders. And it also involves numerous private spheres within which the townsman typically locates the point of his existence. The private focus of his life is an emergent property. Probably this was not noticeable in the first towns, but its spread is coincidental with the growing dominance of towns and the withering away of village culture. The work-oriented model seeks perfection of the village pattern of settlement by enriching the way of life so that while retaining a predominantly public focus it encourages growth and expression of the full range of the inhabitants' capabilities. The leisure-oriented model seeks similar perfection of the town pattern of settlement by enabling people to achieve self-directed growth within lives that are privately focused. The two models are thus intimately tied to the two practices men have evolved regarding the appropriate manner of relating with one another and with their environment.

II

What determines an archaeologist or historian, confronting evidence of a previously unnoticed Roman Britain or Anglo-Saxon settlement, to call it a village rather than a town? The first issue to consider is the importance of size, in the senses of acreage and population. Obviously, the larger the settlement the more likely that it will be thought of as a town. And no doubt at some point size is

1 James Mellaart, *Earliest Civilizations of the Near East* (London, 1965), p. 18. I don't deny that there were *settlements* before the Proto-Neolithic; what this era brings are *permanent* settlements as the *normal* human habitat.

decisive. Thus, the Roman London wall enclosed about 330 acres. Any settlement of that size discovered from the same period would certainly be called a town, regardless of any other features. And at the other extreme, a settlement that enclosed only five acres would probably be regarded as a village for that reason alone. What is of interest, though, as leading to an understanding of the settlements themselves, is the problem created when the settlement uncovered is on the borderline between the largest known Anglo-Saxon villages and the smallest known towns. Imagine a settlement of around thirty acres and a population of five hundred. What sorts of evidence will determine whether it is to be called a village or a town?

Shall we say that what counts is whether the inhabitants are primarily engaged in farming? But it has been argued that agriculture was invented by townspeople who farmed it out to primitive settlements whose inhabitants previously had been food-gatherers, while towns themselves were first made possible by control of the obsidian trade.[2] This is an audacious suggestion, but we cannot reject it on the semantical ground that no place extensively involved in farm work should be called a 'town.' And, from the other side, in some villages the principal occupation is mining.

Nevertheless, farming does seem relevant. When we think of farming as the distinctive activity of villagers rather than of townspeople, we have in mind farming as mainly carried on for the sustenance of the villagers themselves, rather than for purposes of trade. By contrast, town agriculture is thought of as either a sideline or an industry. This suggests that in stressing the association of farming with villages we have in mind farming as grounding a closed style of life, one that involves little commerce with the outside world. Our conception of a town, apart from the matter of size, is of a settlement more open to the outside, and open in a variety of ways, through more than one channel. Thus it is compatible with our conception of a village that it should have a market day when outsiders come for farm products. But although we can accept that the villagers might be dependent on the market and remain villagers, doubts arise in proportion as their relations with outsiders in the marketing context are seen as important and pervasive elements of their way of life. So far as this occurs we will begin to think of them as townspeople. By contrast, when people who inhabit a quite large settlement show no signs of such openness to the outside, we are likely to refer to the place as an overgrown village.

When we call a mining settlement a village we are regarding it in much the way we do a village that has a market day. Mining is its means of livelihood, and the mining activity makes it less insular. But the resulting commerce with the outside world, though a causal condition of its survival as a village, isn't

2 J. Jacobs, *The Economy of Cities* (New York, 1969).

thought of as entering to any extent into its way of life. As soon as we picture the inhabitants as caught up in this commerce – billing accounts, ordering equipment, exporting mined material, negotiating with buyers – we cease to see the settlement as a village.

One of the classical theories concerning the origin of towns is that they were formed for protection from marauders.[3] The idea is that in an inhospitable environment people cluster together for mutual defence. They build a wall around themselves, form an army, and settle down together within their enclosure mainly in order that they may be safe. In so far as it is claimed that the people are protecting themselves, and that the reason for being of the town is mutual protection, the facts don't support the theory. Walls were often built for defence, and people preferred to live within rather than without the walls when the territory outside was traversed by marauders. But by stopping there the theory assumes that the first towns were essentially cut off from their surroundings, turned inward in a defensive posture. This is possible: we may imagine that the settlements engaged in a largely insular, agricultural way of life, and produced sufficient surplus to maintain an army. But it isn't what usually happened. Rather, the military capability possessed – one may say, 'produced' – by the settlement was a service that it sold to the surrounding region, for which it received food and other conditions for its own existence. Such a settlement, one whose function is to defend a region and which prospers as a result of doing this well, is more obviously a town than is one whose military capability is wholly spent in its own defence and which in other respects also is insular.

In part, the claim that 'villages are insular while towns are open to the outside' is terminological. That part is uninteresting. It matters little whether some people call some of the latter kinds of places villages, some of the former towns. 'Town' in particular is used rather differently in England than in Canada, and in New England it has another sense. What does matter is that there are places of these two sorts, that they both began to appear in great numbers during the Proto-Neolithic, and that they underwent the kinds of development described here.

Mellaart, speculating on the sources of Jericho's wealth not long after 8000 B.C., notes that 'Some other source of revenue [than hunting, fishing, or agriculture] must have existed, and this was probably trade. Jericho was well situated for commercial enterprise; it commanded the resources of the Dead Sea, salt, bitumen and sulphur, all useful products in early societies. Obsidian, nephrite and other greenstones from Anatolia, turquoise matrix from Sinai and

3 F.M. Maitland, *Township and Borough* (Cambridge, 1898); H. Pirenne, *Medieval Cities*, trans. F.D. Halsey (Princeton, 1946).

cowries from the Red Sea have been found in the remains of the town, only a fraction of which was excavated.' And though Çatal Hüyük, a bit later, primarily depended on agriculture, there were in the town numerous flourishing and highly developed crafts that depended on materials imported from western Anatolia, Cyprus, the Levant, and Syria.[4] Neither Jericho nor Çatal Hüyük was simply a large, self-contained place, but both prospered through the relations they maintained with an extensive surrounding territory. Functionally this decisively removes them from the 'village' category.

'Insularity' and 'closure' are not honorific terms. 'Self-sufficiency,' by contrast, brings into prominence two features of the village ideal that the other terms hide. The ideal is to establish within the settlement a way of life that is sufficient, complete, in that it answers to the full range of capabilities of the inhabitants. And this completeness is sought in a lifestyle that is essentially collective, one more-or-less continuous fabric of common concerns and pursuits not punctuated by private spheres. The interrelationship of these features can best be seen by considering the development of the ideal in the thought of Plato and Aristotle, the first and still most insightful philosophers of settlements.

III

Plato and Aristotle held that the reason 'cities' are formed is that people aren't self-sufficient. In isolation we are unable to survive, much less live well. By forming a city we create a larger social fact that supplies the self-sufficiency isolated individuals lack. Each is then related to the city so that he contributes to the self-sufficiency of the whole, and receives benefits he is unable to provide by his own efforts, thus overcoming his lack of self-sufficiency.

With Aristotle it was simply a fact that people can't provide all of their own needs and so must enter into relations with others in which each receives benefits produced by the rest. But Plato went beyond this to convert the fact into an ideal. He argued that a person's contribution to the self-sufficiency of the whole city *should* be restricted to that particular special function that his own developed competence best fits him for contributing. Let him who is adept at shoe-making mind his last, and leave the governing to those who do that well. A just city, he held, is one in which this advice is followed – each performs the task he is best equipped by nature and training to perform, which requires that such tasks be open to people, that there be an open system of education in which people are enabled to nurture their native capabilities, and then that people do in fact settle into their appropriate roles. Social injustice consists in these conditions not being fulfilled, with the result that there are numerous

4 *Earliest Civilizations of the Near East*, pp. 36, 84.

square pegs perched unstably over round holes. In the political sphere, democracy is then an unjust institution by definition, since it opens politics to everyone rather than restricting it to those specially qualified.

Aristotle held that man is by nature a political animal, a view with which Plato was in substantial agreement. This meant that a city-state presents the kind of setting in which a person is most likely to develop and find opportunity for expressing his distinctively human capabilities. The city-state is his natural habitat in the same way that low-lying, swampy ground is the natural habitat of many ferns, or sunny, well-drained slopes that of most flowers. A city-state presents the conditions peculiarly favourable for man's growth and life as man. In Aristotle's view a human environment would be one that nurtured and encouraged expression of moral and intellectual virtues – manliness and, for those capable of it, a contemplative life. The challenge to the statesman is to order affairs so that the life of the city expresses these virtues. Thus, we are not to think of the city as a mutually convenient arrangement, an association from which each takes something of benefit to himself. Its value, rather, is more intrinsic: the city grounds a collective life in which each realizes himself as a human. It is therefore a common good in which all share, not as it were a grab bag from which each takes something of value to himself.

Plato and Aristotle were the philosophers of the *polis*. No doubt their own city, Athens, came nowhere near achieving the ideal they formulated. It didn't establish a self-sufficient mode of life for its citizens because its lifestyle was more porous than the ideal contemplated. In addition, it failed to achieve the richness of opportunity required of an environment that is to objectify the full range of human potentiality. Finally, by restricting rights of citizenship to a select minority of the population, it failed by perpetuating massive social injustice. In many ways, these failures were matched by defects in the philosophers' theories. Aristotle endorsed slavery and the withholding of rights of citizenship from many other classes of persons as well – from women and 'mechanics,' for example – and Plato's enthusiasm for 'justice' in the sense of everyone staying in the place he is fitted to occupy was certainly unbalanced.

If we abstract from these failings we are left with one large ideal of enduring merit, that of a self-contained settlement which grounds a way of life that allows man to live as man.[5] The village bias of the ideal is shown by its stress

5 'These considerations indicate clearly the optimum standard of population. It is, in a word, "the greatest surveyable number required for achieving a life of self-sufficiency" ... Similar considerations apply also to the matter of territory. So far as the *character* of the soil is concerned, everybody would obviously give the preference to a territory which ensured the maximum of self-sufficiency; and as that consists in having everything, and needing nothing, such a territory must be one which produces all kinds of crops. In point of *extent* and size, the territory should be large enough to enable its

on the self-containment of the way of life and on its collective character, a more prominent feature in Plato than in Aristotle. In one respect there is no arguing with the ideal: it can scarcely be denied that a person ought to find his environment conducive to development and expression of his distinctive potentialities. What is arguable is what those potentialities are, whether it is sensible to seek to build such an environment within a confined settlement, and whether the way of life it establishes should be predominantly collective.

IV

The distinctive feature of the town as a pattern of settlement is that it is open to the outside. It is open in the sense that it is interdependent with life outside its boundaries, and also in the sense that the town lifestyle involves transactions with the outside world. No doubt towns and town culture possessed these traits from the very beginning. But initially, in village and town alike, people probably apprehended the point of their existence to consist in their integral, collective life. The history of villages in our era, and of the transformation of settlements from a village to a town form, is largely one of places losing this integrity. We associate the change with dissolution of villages, but with growth of towns. Private spheres opened up within settlements and gradually grew in importance until a nearly total reversal of emphasis from the public to the private sphere occurred.

From a situation where private spheres and a private life were incidents accorded no great importance in the overall order, and the collective life of the settlement per se was the central value and the centre of gravity in the lives of the inhabitants, we have evolved a situation in which in the original sense the settlement has no 'collective life per se'; and institutionalization of extensive private spheres is matched by institutionalization of the merely instrumental value of the practices that once had formed that collective life.

To grasp the idea of a private sphere, and its contrast with a collective life to which intrinsic significance is accorded, we may think of a primitive form of settlement, a tribal village. Consider it as located in a clearing, a circle of one-room huts in which thirty or forty families live. The women of the village cook and look after the children at the front of their huts, within the open circle whose perimeter is formed by the huts themselves. During the day the men of the village go off together to hunt or to farm. The evening meal is eaten in front of the hut, in close proximity to and in full sight of one's neighbours, and when it is time to retire all members of the family bed down together in

inhabitants to live a life of leisure which combines liberality with temperance' 1326b. *The Politics of Aristotle*, trans. E. Barker (Oxford, 1946), pp. 292-3.

the one open room that forms their home. It is obvious that here there is little distinction between a public and a private sphere. But though there is little *privacy*, not all of the functions carried out in public are public in character. Thus, hunting, as we have imagined it, is a public, communal function – an activity of the village at large – but nevertheless there is a family life, involving at a minimum care of the children, cooking, eating, sleeping, and sexual activity. By and large, the tribe is the family writ large. The public-private distinction refers to the size of the group that is responsible for a practice and that has rights in the results of carrying it out. Thus, hunting is a tribal activity while routine cooking occurs in a private, family sphere. This suggests that members of the tribe co-ordinate their individual activities when hunting, but not when cooking. And if an individual single-handedly makes a kill the entire tribe asserts a right in the flesh and skin, while the results of cooking are regarded as 'property' of the family responsible.

In some instances we would regard the co-ordination or lack of co-ordination of effort as the crucial feature that determines whether a practice is public or private relative to the settlement within which it is carried out. In other instances we would regard the attitude concerning rights in the results of the activity as decisive. We are likely to think of hunting as occurring in the public sphere, even though individual members of the tribe hunt independently of one another, since the kill is treated as communal property in the first instance and not a possession of the person who made the kill. But if activities in connection with preparing meals were co-ordinated throughout the tribe, we would probably regard them as public, as occurring in the public sphere, regardless of the way in which rights in the co-operatively prepared food were allocated.

The distinction between privacy and the private sphere is that between knowledge and authority. Thus, members of the tribe carry out private acts, such as cooking, without privacy. The lack of privacy consists in the fact that what they are doing is known or readily knowable by all. The private character of the act, by contrast, involves the fact that despite this knowledge the others aren't to interfere. They have no authority over the form of the activity, which is determined by the family not the tribe, or over the results of the activity, which are treated as family property. But this relation of privacy with the private sphere implies that they are likely to go together, since actions that are carried out in privacy, without the knowledge of others, cannot be effectively controlled by others – their imputed authority cannot be made effective. Consequently, the development of privacy in a sphere of life leads to its conversion to a private sphere. From the other side, however, introduction of publicity does not with the same inevitability lead to conversion to a public sphere.

The tribal village presents one extreme: a way of life that possesses little privacy, a subtle blend of private and public spheres, so that where one shades into the other is not readily discernible, with the bulk of life and the affairs of greatest moment located in the public sphere. At the other extreme, consider a modern city. Here the public-private distinction is sharper, the private sphere is considerably wider, and the public sphere exists largely as a means for the sustenance and decoration of the private, so that the centre of gravity of the settlement rests securely in the latter domain. Rather than illustrate this contrast statically, by referring to features of contemporary cities, I shall discuss five developments in the history of towns and villages that exhibit particular ways in which the shift from a primarily public-focused to a private-focused settlement came about.

1 Village communities in England typically were built around or in association with a manor that was the focus of the settlement. In Anglo-Saxon times the manor was a quasi-public facility rather than a private dwelling for the lord of the manor. The lord was a military chieftain and the manor was a facility that he used in performing that function. The centre of the manor was the great hall, where many communal functions involving numerous persons other than members of the lord's immediate family were carried out. It was a place to sleep, cook, eat, hold court, entertain, and administer village affairs. An important chapter in the history of domestic architecture would describe the process by which the functions carried out in the multi-purpose room came to be differentiated and to acquire distinctive and specially designed facilities. Some of these changes involved articulation of spaces in the house itself – creation of dining rooms and bedrooms – and some involved the transfer of a function that had been carried on in the great hall to a structure located elsewhere in the village. In the end, the multi-purpose hall became a sitting room, one function among others and private in character. The development can be traced in particular manors: cellars converted into dining rooms, other spaces partitioned off to become bedrooms, so that gradually over the centuries the same structure that first served a largely public purpose became the shell of domesticity.

2 A second development in the village community, and one of considerably greater significance, was the elimination of the open field system. The process of enclosure in England over the period between 1700 and 1850 is often credited with having destroyed the village community itself. The original open fields of the village communities were of three sorts, all sometimes referred to as 'commons': the arable, laid out in strips encircling the village; the waste; and the pasture or meadow. The waste and meadow were public ground to which by and large all had access. The arable strips were semi-public. Particular indi-

viduals controlled them; a farmer might 'own' a number of strips located at various points around the village, totalling perhaps thirty acres. But critical decisions regarding their use were collectively made: which strips would lie fallow and which would be cultivated in any given year; also the times of planting, harvesting, and of converting the arable to pasture, when the strips would revert to the status of public property. Enclosure consisted of dividing the commons into parcels of private property, thus eliminating the historic rights of the community in the land.

No doubt some enclosures were defensible in the circumstances. Over time the historic rights of a community often had become in effect the private rights of a few who through their control of the commons forced others to live in crowded conditions and blocked desirable developments. Nottingham and Stamford, for example, were both strangled by a commons that encircled the town. In Nottingham a lovely seventeenth-century town became two centuries later a squalid city. Outward growth was inhibited by a handful of families who, possessing the rights in the commons surrounding the city, were able to forestall enclosure for two hundred years. In Stamford a single individual, Lord Exeter, who saw enclosure as a threat to his political power, was the obstacle, while the community at large found the commons an inhibiting feudal relic.[6]

By contrast, other and perhaps most enclosures served private interests and worked against the well-being of the communities affected. For the most part, these were enclosures of commons that surrounded settlements which had retained their traditional character and were not in the path of industrial development. But however one assesses the enclosure movement, it clearly shifted the focus of farm life in the villages from the public to the private sphere, and by doing so it eliminated the village community as the dominant form of English settlement. In a village community the surrounding commons was the locus of the working day. It gave a predominantly public focus to that portion of the inhabitants' lives. Farming was in many respects a community activity. Moreover, the openness of the fields, and their partition into narrow strips with no high hedges between, meant that a family working its own strips stood side by side with those working adjoining land, so that not only was the activity less private than it became later but also those carrying it out did so in less privacy. Elimination of the commons meant elimination of the principal solid basis for active community in the villages. Since in that setting work was the focus of existence, its privatization meant the privatization of village life.

3 Typically, towns in England were market towns, and their focal point was a large space at the centre where the market was located. Hence the 'porosity'

6 W.G. Hoskins, *The Making of the English Landscape* (London, 1955), chap. 9.

of town life: the market is a facility not simply for the town itself but for a region, and establishes the town as a centre for its region. The market place is a public facility – an open space that facilitates interaction among townspeople and between townspeople and outsiders. In larger places, London, for example, the marketing function was considerably less localized. Most of the streets of the city provided market space: Poultry Street, Floral Street, Cheapside, Cornhill, Leadenhall, Milk Street, Bread Street, Bow Lane, etc.

It is interesting that at present the provincial town is the natural home of the supermarket and the large metropolis of more specialized shops, so that shopping in the latter is notoriously more time-consuming. This contrast parallels the earlier one between the centralized market of the small town and the diffused market streets of the large cities. In effect, in provincial towns the market place was roofed over and became an enclosed supermarket, a conversion of public space into private and elimination from the town of a public function that supported its communal character in the same way that the open fields supported community in the villages. In large cities, the roofing over consisted of bringing the diffuse market in off the streets to the buildings that line them – the creation of roofed over and enclosed shops – thus retaining the pattern of diffusion that from the beginning distinguished the city with its street markets from the provincial town with its central market place, but following the same pattern of conversion of land use from public to private functions.

The earlier, open marketing, whether centralized or diffuse, was the occasion for extensive social interaction, a community activity in a public setting. Street cries and haggling over prices may be contrasted with K-Mart P.A. announcements of bargains at the notions counter. The latter suggests an instrumental activity. Its point will be experienced elsewhere, at home when the purchases are put to use. The former indicates a way of life, an activity which is sensed to have intrinsic meaning.

4 Next, consider a different dimension of the structure of family life and trade. The earlier pattern, in towns as well as villages, involved no sharp separation of work from family life. In the village most members of the family would be found in the fields at one time or another, and many elements of what we think of as work life were carried on within the home. The significance of this integration of family and work varies, depending on whether it occurs on a self-sufficient homestead or in a village with an economy in which work is a social activity – that is, a village that produces socially in the sense that the production of each is consumed by all. On a homestead integration has no implications for the private character of family life – however important it may be in other respects – since work no more involves an essential relationship

with a larger whole than do family affairs. But in the village the effect of integration is to soften the sense and reality of a separation between the public and private spheres. In the flow of family life the passage from what we regard as the more distinctively family functions – cooking, eating, sleeping, child rearing, and intimacy – to farm work is a natural one. When the one sort of activities follows the other it is not readily obvious where the first leaves off and the second starts up; and often both sorts are going on at the same time and in the same activities: working the fields is also an aspect of educating the children, churning the butter a manifestation of intimacy. In these circumstances, interpenetration of work and family life means at once that work life is more private and family life more public than we know them to be.

One of the most profound developments over the past four hundred years has been the splitting off of work and family life.[7] This development is not to be identified with the passage from feudalism to capitalism, since in the villages the early capitalist pattern of cottage industries involved renewed unification of work and family; but there can be no question that as capitalist production progressed the separation of the two institutions became far greater than was experienced in previous eras. In the village communities the collapse of the open field system contributed to the separation, as did consolidation of farm ownership into fewer hands, greater use of day labour on the farms, and the practice of farming as a secondary occupation carried on by people who also worked as industrial labourers. The result in the villages was that family life increasingly became a domain of privacy from the outside world, within which life had little public significance. The boundaries between this sphere and the public domain became readily discernible, and a social expectation developed that the boundaries would be respected.

In the towns a similar development occurred. Guild organization of production and trade meant that commerce and industry were often a dimension of family life. But the relationship perhaps served more to give public character to family life than to domesticize industry, for it meant that the 'family' for many purposes included not merely the guild master and his wife, children, and servants, but his journeymen and apprentices as well.

5 Finally, we should consider a political development. The received theory of political democracy holds that the object of government is to satisfy the interests of the governed and that this should be accomplished through institutions that enable the governed to influence the direction of governmental policy. The influence may make itself felt in various ways. These form the various 'kinds' of democracy: direct, the governed functioning as the government by

7 See especially P. Laslett, *The World We Have Lost* (New York, 1965), pp. 13-21.

actually making the critical decisions; by referendum, which is direct democracy from a distance; representative, decisions taken by persons whose interests, officially at any rate, reflect the interests of a portion of the electorate, so that a legislative body exists that maps the distribution of interests in the population at large; and by recall, the capability of replacing the government in case a majority of the governed do not find their interests adequately reflected in the decisions taken. The key idea through these forms of democracy is that the interests of the governed, or of the majority of them, should predominate. For 'interests' we may put 'what they want,' or their preferences. In a society that has achieved a marked distinction between public and private spheres, a distinction between public and private preferences also develops. If it is found that a person wants something or other, say, a higher salary, then we may wonder whether this is a private preference or a public one.[8] That is, we may wonder whether this is a condition that he prefers as producing a benefit in his individual life or some private sphere in which he is involved, on one hand, or, on the other, as producing a benefit for the community at large. The standard theory of democracy, which is largely reflected in democratic practice, holds that the interests the theory refers to are private preferences. The rationale for this is that the public interest is in fact nothing more than the sum of private preferences, so that if indeed institutions are established that secure satisfaction of most of the private preferences of the population, then automatically the public interest will have been satisfied.

Over the past few centuries political institutions have been developed that are highly responsive to private interests, institutions which, when working well, result in public policies that systematically satisfy the maximum number of preferences. Thus, political parties are often identified by the cluster of private preferences they respond to, and as many see it the 'business of politics' is that of working out packages of programs for satisfying coalitions of interest groups, with the object of catching up sufficient strength by way of votes and financial support to be elected to office. For example, a farm policy is an attempt to bring in the support of farmers and in working out such a policy the problem is to frame it so that it doesn't alienate other interest groups whose support is also sought. If one objects that such an approach sacrifices the interest of the whole community in a scramble for votes the answer is that the well-being of the whole community is assured to the degree that the coalition formed by the successful party does in fact satisfy the private preferences of the population. The historical development that underlies this political

8 The character of this distinction, and the circumstances in which it is important that it be observed, are considered with some care in Brian Barry, *Political Argument* (London, 1965).

theory and practice is emergence within the community of a sharp distinction between public and private spheres, and relegation of the former to the status of an instrument, a means of satisfying the latter, rather than a domain where intrinsic values are found. Neither the theory nor the practice would have been possible in a traditional village community, since the institutional conditions for its formulation didn't exist there.

V

The contrast between village and town is essentially one between a pattern of life in which no sharp differentiation between a private and a public sphere is institutionalized and in which life is principally focused on the public sphere, on the one hand, and, on the other, a pattern in which such a differentiation is very sharp indeed and in which the focus of life is on the private sphere. The dissolution of the village community is largely a process of emphasizing the private sphere, and the growth of towns into large metropolises exhibits a similar progression. It comes as no surprise, therefore, that in the dispute between partisans of villages and large cities, the latter complain about lack of privacy in small places and the former about the anonymity of life in cities. Nor shall we be surprised to learn in the next chapter that the philosophical systems that in effect justify urban living stress the distinction between the public and private spheres and argue that the latter should be as wide as possible.

The self-sufficient village mode of life, in relation with the outside world, brought insularity; internally it brought collective integrity, oneness, and wholeness. Growth and institutionalization of private spheres undermined both features: opened the village to the outside and fragmented the continuous fabric of its lifestyle. Wholists seem seduced above all by the oneness of the fabric, not the insularity, while it is the insularity that appears to preclude the individual development and independence that individualists cherish. What history has not shown us is a pattern of living in which the public sphere dominates, but that is not insular but open to the world. Perhaps it is with such a pattern that the hope for the future rests.

CHAPTER SIX

Hegel and Mill

The work-oriented model expresses a wholistic, and the leisure-oriented model an individualistic, world-view. In the preceding chapter the contrast between these was seen through the opposition between essential features of village and town: self-sufficiency as opposed to openness, and the more-or-less continuous fabric of a self-contained life as opposed to a lifestyle marked by extensive private spheres. The idea is that from the beginning of settled life, not much more than ten thousand years ago, these two patterns of settlement have coexisted as opposed institutional expressions of how men wish to live. In this perspective the work-oriented and leisure-oriented models are as deeply rooted in human experience as they could possibly be, since they are inspired by visions of the perfected form of the two patterns of settlement.

In this chapter I shall consider the ideational side of the contrast. Our intellectual history presents us with strands of thought which, on various levels of abstraction, have the effect of justifying one or the other of the two points of view. In planning literature the debate between urbanists and ruralists has been going on for nearly a century - evidence, perhaps, that the issue is more philosophical than technical - and rather basic principles of settlement design are at stake. In the literary tradition partisans of rural life have predominated. Emerson's essay, *Farming*, is a classic statement. But 'urbanism' had a powerful spokesman in William Blake who vehemently rejected Wordsworth's conviction that nature, 'the universe,' fits and fulfils human nature. And even in classical times, although the basic tenor of Aristotle's as well as Plato's political thought is sympathetic with distinguishing features of the village pattern, most of the specific contrasts between the two show Aristotle as moving toward an urban ideal. He attacks Plato's collectivism as not conducive to the development of individuality and defends private property on the same basis. And in terms of patterns of social living idealized by both, perhaps the most significant contrast is that ideally Plato's *polis* would be a place where everyone contributes to the smooth functioning of the whole (so that it is basically a city of work) while in Aristotle's ideal city work is done primarily in order that some may enjoy leisure in the specific form of contemplative activity.

Philosophy in the modern era is generally written at a level of generality somewhat above that on which such terms as 'city,' 'village,' 'work,' and 'leisure' appear. Instead, one reads of 'society,' 'the state,' and 'activity.' Consequently, wholist and individualist tendencies don't show up in the form of explicit arguments for a work or leisure orientation, or in defence of either the village or the urban pattern of settlement. Nevertheless, political and social philosophy of the past two hundred years has not been irrelevant to the debates in the planning literature or to the clash of sentiments expressed in the literary tradition.

Perhaps the three most influential political and social philosophers of the nineteenth century were Hegel, Marx, and John Stuart Mill. Each developed a distinctive perspective on human life that has profound bearing on the leisure-oriented and work-oriented models. Primarily this results from their defending principles that ground values to which these two models appeal. The significance of Marx's thought in this regard will be considered in Chapter 9. With respect to Mill and Hegel, one could not label them respectively as the philosophers of leisure and work. But if they had chosen to cast their political and social thought at that more concrete level at which these terms have a natural application it seems clear that this would have been the contrast between them.

This is not the place to attempt a comprehensive, balanced statement of these two philosophies. What is important, instead, is to see something of the kinds of very general ideas that support the leisure- and work-oriented models. Thus, it is certain ideas embedded in the thought of Mill and Hegel, not their systems as a whole, or even their thought as such, that we must look to.[1] Inevitably, then, there will be some wrenching of ideas from their intended context. The risks inherent in the procedure will have been worth bearing if we gain insight into the more abstract form of the contrast that is met institution-

1 The relevant texts for these purposes are Hegel's *Lectures on the Philosophy of History* and *Philosophy of Right*; and Mill's *On Liberty*, *Utilitarianism*, and *Principles of Political Economy*. The *flavour* of Hegel's thought, particularly regarding freedom and the relation of the individual to *Geist* and to the natural environment, is most readily obtained from his introduction to *Philosophy of History*. Mill's argument for the basic libertarian view is in *On Liberty*; the more abstract ethical theory, and the argument by which he translates the notion that pleasure is the only good into the view that the more important goods are those associated with exercise of our 'higher faculties,' are found in *Utilitarianism*; more concrete social and economic applications are worked out in *Principles of Political Economy*. A useful secondary source for Hegel's political philosophy is a volume of essays edited by Z.A. Pelczynski, *Hegel's Political Philosophy* (Cambridge, 1971). See especially the contributions by Pelczynski and J. Plamenatz.

ally in cities and villages and imaginatively in the idealizations of a leisure- and a work-oriented existence.

II

Three interrelated principles argued for by Mill form a natural basis for both the individualistic outlook and the model of a leisure-oriented society. These principles provide criteria for rightness, goodness, and possession of a right. The first principle identifies the conditions under which an act is 'right'; the second, those under which a life is 'good'; the third, those under which an individual has 'a right.' The first is the principle of utility; the second, that of individuality; the third, that of equal freedom. The first supports the ideal of a humanized technology; the second grounds an individualistic lifestyle; the third yields an argument for the extension of leisure. Mill himself was only partly aware of these uses of his principles.

1 Of the three principles, the first is the most widely understood and discussed. According to it, the rightness of an action is a function of its utility, that is, of its tendency to have good consequences for human life. There are just two features of interest in the principle of utility: first, it makes the rightness of an action depend on the consequences of carrying it out; second, the only consequences that bear on the rightness of an action are those that bring *human* benefits. Because of the first feature the principle of utility is future-oriented; because of the second it is humanistic.

To appreciate the significance of the principle, notice what it rules out as being irrelevant to the rightness of an action. Among the alternatives to the first feature are willingness to allow certain relationships of an action with past events to influence the decision concerning its rightness, and a willingness to be influenced by some characteristics of the action itself, as opposed to its consequences. Some of the relationships with the past that have been thought relevant in this connection are those suggested by the ideas of loyalty, making reparations and restitution, and sticking to one's promises. The distinction between being influenced by characteristics of the action itself and being sensitive only to its effects is that in the first case intrinsic value is attributed to the act and in the latter case only instrumental value. In effect, in the first case one is asking whether the act is fit to stand as an element in an ideal whole. There is a difference between the fitness of an action to constitute an ideal whole and its tendency to build such a whole as a consequence. Thus, we may regard acts of violence as contributory to an ideal whole but may nevertheless conceive that whole so that violence has no place in it. The point of the non-utilitarian alternative is that it leaves open the possibility that the fact an action is unfit to constitute an ideal whole is of more weight than the fact it contributes to such a whole, although in an unworthy manner – the possibility, as it is misleadingly put, of an end that doesn't justify its means.

The alternative to the humanistic feature of the principle of utility is to hold that there are goods that don't peculiarly refer to men. In the second chapter I referred to the view that the survival of species of life other than man is such a good – that is, the view that we ought to make an effort to secure the survival of such species, not just because of benefit that comes or might come to men from their continued existence, but as well because their survival is seen as valuable in itself. Given such a broadened view of good it is possible to conceive the ideal whole one's actions ought to contribute to and ought to be fit to constitute as one in which men have a place but not as one wholly formed for human benefit.

The humanistic and future-oriented features of the principle of utility make it a natural foundation for the ideal of a humanized technology. To humanize a technology is to assure that the consequences of its application work for human benefit. Pursuing this as a goal is an alternative to seeking to minimize the bad effects of a technology simply by refusing to apply it. The principle of utility doesn't *logically* imply either of these attitudes toward technology. If more human benefit would result from restricting rather than controlling technology then that is the course to follow. Nevertheless, the advocate of humanizing technology structures the problem in just the way favoured by the utilitarian. One who evaluates a practice with the principle of utility in mind will look first to its consequences, asking how far they are beneficial to human life. To find that the practice isn't as desirable as it might be is to find that its consequences aren't as beneficial as they might be. And the challenge to improve matters is seen in the first instance as that of improving the consequences – of 'humanizing' them. The idea of eliminating the practice, or of drastically curtailing it, is shunted in last in this priority of concerns.

On the other hand, those who oppose technology may do so on utilitarian grounds but need not. There is likely to be a non-utilitarian bias to their case, in the fundamental sense that their distrust of technology manifests distrust of the utilitarian's way of structuring social problems. Technology and science are of course associated, and to be 'anti-technology' is generally to be anti-science as well. Utilitarianism is a form of the ideal that one should be 'scientific' in resolving social problems, and is often seen as the foundation for a technology of social improvement.

2 What is of special interest here are the links between the principle of utility, endorsement of a leisure-oriented society, and rejection of the ideal of community. The sequence of ideas in Mill is roughly as follows. The only conse-

quences that should count in deciding the utility of an act are those that involve satisfaction or dissatisfaction – of needs, interests, or preferences. In fleshing out the idea of human satisfaction, however, Mill finally emphasizes the satisfaction of an interest in expressing and developing 'higher' human faculties – creativity, sensitivity, intellectual endeavour, moral sensibility – on the basis that people who have experienced the satisfactions associated with these activities consistently prefer them over the pleasures of other endeavours: better to be a Socrates dissatisfied than a pig satisfied. The result is that as Mill develops the conception of good incorporated in the principle of utility, from being the simple formula that good equals human benefit or satisfaction it becomes the proposition that a good life for the individual is one in which he develops and expresses his capabilities to the fullest, and in particular his highest capabilities. When he turns to the evaluation of social institutions, in *On Liberty* and *The Principles of Political Economy*, the evaluative principle he employs is that of self-realization: the test of an institution is the degree to which it fosters individual growth.

Of course, to adopt a conception of the good that stresses individual growth does not automatically bias one toward an individualistic and away from a communal life style. It only establishes growth as the criterion for success of the latter. What especially determines the individualistic character of Mill's conception of the good is his further elaboration of the conditions for individual growth. In this connection he stressed, above all other factors, the importance of personal decision. He argued that for a person to develop his distinctive capabilities he should be frequently called upon to make up his own mind so that his actions reflect personal decision and are not coerced by legal rules or social pressure. Stress on this condition for growth, largely to the exclusion of all others, led Mill to place great value on spontaneity and eccentricity, so much so that in discussing the possibility that communism is 'the ultimate form of social organization' he let the case rest on the issue of whether communism or capitalism 'is consistent with the greatest amount of human liberty and spontaneity.'[2] Although he appears to be undecided as to which would best satisfy the test, and speaks of the need for experimentation with communism to gain an empirical basis for a decision, the criterion he recommends for considering the issue fairly well settles the matter in favour of the individualistic alternative. A general stress on the importance of freedom would not create the bias, since it is open to us to construe freedom in different ways. But by associating freedom with spontaneity, eccentricity, and independence of judgment, Mill assigns top priority to a condition more readily assured by an individualistic than by a communal lifestyle. There is room for spontaneity within

2 *Principles of Political Economy* (3rd ed., London, 1852), I, pp. 255, 256.

community, to be sure, but since the community depends on certain practices being generally followed it is necessary that the spontaneity express itself in endorsement of those practices. Thus, we can imagine the farmers in a village community spontaneously going to their fields each morning and spontaneously doing their chores in the traditional way. But there is tension in this fortuitous combination of community and spontaneity, since if the spontaneity is genuine at any moment it may reflect itself in other decisions which would undermine the community. An individualistic lifestyle, involving real mutual independence, so that the fate of the settlement is not at stake with each individual exercise of spontaneity, is a more appropriate ordering of human affairs for anyone who emphasizes, as Mill does, the importance of individual decision for personal growth.

If we take the perspective of a person participating in a social arrangement, it is clear that Mill was mistaken in representing his principle as not biasing the choice between communism and 'free enterprise.' With what sympathy will one who feels the prime importance of independence of judgment and spontaneity view the 'discipline' of community life? He will see that a condition of community well-being is that he conduct himself in certain ways. But so far as he values spontaneity he will want always to find that the determinant of his choices is some inward element, a wholly *self*-originated sense that what he is doing is appropriate, or fun, or needful, or good, rather than an externally derived realization that it is *called for* by the order of life within which he finds himself.

3 The idea of having a right is that of having access to a sphere of action within which a person is free in the sense that how he conducts himself is altogether his own affair, not subject to regulation by others. Consequently, it is also a sphere within which he enjoys power over others, since the freedom it involves is enforceable. Having the right involves having authority to demand that others refrain from interfering with its exercise. On one hand, the sphere of individual rights is the domain of a person's life not subject to control by others. On the other, it is the domain within which he may rightfully control the actions of others. Thus, my right to worship marks off a sphere of activity in which I may express my religious feelings without interference, and at the same time establishes my authority to restrain others who seek to interfere with such expression. To possess a home as property is to be free to use and enjoy the home as one chooses – to the extent that the property rights specify – and it is to have authority to close the door on everyone who would infringe the property rights.[3]

3 The fact that the primary significance of having a right is that it bestows authority to interfere with others is elaborated by H.L.A. Hart in 'Are There Any Natural Rights?' *Philosophical Review*, LXIV (1955).

The distinction, then, between the sphere of a person's rights and the sphere in which he has no distinctive rights is that between a private and a public sphere. The avowed purpose of *On Liberty* is to defend a principle on the basis of which these two spheres may be staked out – as Mill states it, the sphere subject to social control and the sphere properly exempt from social control. Note the connection between an interest in formulating such a principle and the evolution of private spheres in settlements.

Mill argues that the only good reason society can have for interfering with the liberty of action of one of its members is self-defence, which amounts to the claim that if the individual is not likely to injure others by his action society ought not to interfere with him. The interest of the person interfered with is not an adequate reason. Thus, a law that requires people to fasten their seat belts, or on motorcycles to wear helmets, cannot be defended by the claim that it would protect people from injuring themselves but must be based on the danger of injury to others. Mill's principle leads to the idea that for the most part the role of government is analogous to that of an umpire. Social interactions should primarily be regulated by the one rule that it is a violation for people to injure one another. Action unlikely to fall foul of that rule generally speaking is not subject to regulation. Rather, it lies in the private sphere, the sphere of rights.

The first impression that this assigns to government an excessively limited role may be corrected by recalling that to have a right is to have power to control others. In a society where there are many rights, large private spheres, there must also be considerable authority. Since exercise of this authority is delegated to government – the individual does not typically enforce his own rights but calls upon the government to do so for him – there must be a proportionately large public sphere. But in these circumstances the public sphere exists for the sake of the private sphere. If we contemplate a society that mainly satisfies Mill's principle the image we get is of a collection of individuals caught up in predominantly private affairs that have no essential impact on the community at large, each enjoying his rights and pursuing his own good. Exercising our rights involves making frequent choices, employing our distinctive capabilities in the act of choosing, following out the implications of those choices on our own initiative, and learning even from our mistakes. The object throughout is individual growth and development, and the principal stress is on the indispensability of self-directedness as a condition of growth.

It would be difficult to find a more natural basis for the ideal of a leisure-oriented society. For the idea of leisure is at bottom that of a life directed by an interest in individual growth or enjoyment, rather than by social need. Mill offers the basic principle of social organization for a society that pursues this interest. When we move from the theory to the society that accepts the theory as an adequate manner of representing its aspirations, then from a theorist who wishes to establish a principle of rights, we come to a group of people who think it important to assert their rights, to stake the claims that the rights entail. This involves asserting authority over others, not to dominate them but to exclude them from one's own sphere. For such a society a life without work, a situation where society doesn't need any particular contribution from the individual as a condition of its well-being, must seem a compelling ideal. It involves elimination of the principal occasion for people injuring one another. To free the society from dependence on particular contributions by the individual is to make it less dependent on the ways he expresses his freedom. As a result, his sphere of rights, the private sphere, may be enlarged beyond anything imaginable in a society focused on work.

III

Leisure, individualism, liberty, spontaneity, privacy, rights, growth, independence of judgment, are all highly honorific terms. Any theory that makes extensive use of such terms is likely to command instant sympathy. It will be considerably more difficult to portray its philosophical alternative in an equally sympathetic light.

I shall begin with an undoubted fact. In stressing the roles of individual choice and action on that choice in fostering self-development, Mill was telling only part of the story. Had he taken a more generous view of the conditions for growth he would have been led to themes that do not support the principle of individual rights in the bald form he gave it. A person's self-development is obviously enhanced by his often being called upon to make up his own mind and accept personal responsibility. But it is equally necessary that the setting in which a person acts and lives be of a certain kind. The part of the truth Mill ignored, or at least didn't make adequate use of, is that people develop their capacities by meeting significant challenges that are neither unmanageable nor excessively easy. This requires that the social context of action have characteristics that may require political policies incompatible with the view of government as, in effect, an umpire.

In broad historical terms, it is the institutional setting of their lives that explains the contrast between the character types found in a modern city and those found in a mediaeval village community. I alluded earlier to the estimate that such a villager may well have seen no more than one or two hundred other human beings in his lifetime, most of whom would have been people very like himself. In such circumstances he will have been called upon to respond to a very restricted range of challenges. The resources and institutional development necessary for more elaborate challenges, without which a more elaborate development of human potential was impossible, did not exist. Consider the implications for his mental development of the fact that the villager's vocabulary consisted of a few hundred words. Limitations of language foster limitations of thought and even feeling, since most feelings have a pronounced conceptual component, and the scope and tone of thoughts and feelings above all fix the quality of life.

The level of institutional development determines the kinds of challenges a person confronts and their manageability. People may learn from failure, certainly, but they don't learn the skills associated with carrying out the activity they are challenged to perform. Success must be possible. There are many settings of human life in which people meet no challenge to create music. One domain of human attainment is thus denied them. The fact that there are no laws prohibiting music counts for very little. Nor would it help matters much simply to introduce some musical instruments, since the challenge these created would not be manageable.

If it is a condition of growth that people are not always told what to do but must decide for themselves and act on their decisions, it is no less a condition that the setting of life presents manageable challenges, which requires a certain kind of institutional development and some measure of order. The factor Mill stressed suggests the desirability of an open, permissive environment, with little external direction; the last-mentioned factor points up the importance of certain substantive features *in* that environment.

As Hegel developed this theme he was led to formulate a conception of freedom that stands in sharp contrast to Mill's. For Mill freedom consists in the absence of restraints, so-called 'negative freedom.'[4] Thus, the liberties he stressed in *On Liberty* - freedom of thought and discussion, liberty of association, and liberty of tastes and pursuits - were all conceived in terms of non-interference. In arguing *for* freedom of thought and discussion he was arguing *against* censorship. 'Liberty of tastes and pursuits' meant not being coerced in one's likes and dislikes and in choice of a career by legal rules or social pressure. When freedom is understood as the absence of legal and social constraints, the tactic of freedom is the simple one of eliminating the constraints. No positive institutional developments and resources are required. At any given time, negative freedom is wholly achievable by removing the constraints then imposed. If freedom in this negative sense is valued more or less to the exclusion of all other conditions, the only basis for limiting the freedom of one person will be that it is necessary to keep him from interfering with the freedom of

4 The history of this concept of 'negative freedom' and of its juxtaposition with 'positive freedom' is relevant to the contrast developed here. See, especially, Isaiah Berlin, 'Two Concepts of Liberty,' in *Four Essays on Liberty* (Oxford, 1969); also B. Bosanquet, *The Philosophical Theory of the State* (London, 1958), pp. 138-44.

another – that is, we will be led to something like Mill's principle of individual rights as the major principle of legislation and rule of social conduct.

But when one notices the importance of institutional development to human growth, the necessity that civilized and civilizing institutions be evolved, it is natural to express this insight in a more positive conception of freedom. If our underlying image is of the person being as it were bottled up, requiring a congenial setting that offers the conditions peculiarly favourable for development and expression of his human potential, then we will see the process by which that setting evolves, which for Hegel means the course of human history, as one during which men *become* free. The sense of the term 'free' here shifts, as a result of a different perspective on the relation of the person with his environment. The dominating analogy is that of biological growth, under the assumption that the growing thing has a nature which in the course of development unfolds. It is the idea that what develops, the mature condition, was there implicitly from the start, with an impulse to blossom forth, but that it required conditions favourable for its appearance. So far as the favourable conditions aren't present, the potentiality won't release itself. It is suppressed by an inhospitable environment. In this context, provision of the required conditions for growth is the 'freeing' of the growing subject. Man is thought of as having a nature with an impetus to develop itself, and growth is seen as a process of self-revelation that naturally follows upon replacement of unfavourable conditions by those that are congenial. There is still the underlying idea of the elimination of constraints, of become 'free' as a matter of being released – a mechanical analogy would be that of releasing the catch on a jack-in-the-box – but now the broadened understanding of what the constraints are gives the conception a predominantly positive thrust. The conditions favourable for growth are features that must be added to the setting.[5]

This more positive view of freedom casts doubt on the goal of a permissive society, marked by few external rules and social pressures. It suggests the desirability of specific institutional developments occurring. One who takes an essentially passive attitude toward the required developments, as Hegel for the most part did, may see them as fated to evolve, and simply await their appearance. A manipulator may expand the positive understanding of freedom into a program for action that points to the steps to be taken in order that the required developments might be carried through. The reforming side of Marx's philosophy is grounded in this aggressive interpretation of positive freedom.

5 Although Hegel uses different categories in discussing *change* than did Aristotle, his basic position is Aristotelian: it is teleological in much the same sense, and it similarly blends a normative with a descriptive account. The main difference is that while Aristotle confined his account to the development of individuals, Hegel applied it to the development of species. He was thus led to conceive a 'science' that Aristotle, perhaps rightly, didn't envisage, the philosophy of history.

Mill's negative view of freedom leads to an individualistic outlook and high regard for leisure. Hegel's more positive view is sympathetic with a communitarian outlook in a work-oriented society. To apply the more positive view it is necessary to have a conception of human nature and of the institutional setting that will best serve as the system of favourable conditions for the unfolding of that nature. However these questions are answered in detail, it is plausible to conclude that man is in a fundamental sense a social creature, that a mode of life that does not involve close interpersonal relationships is something less than fully human. And we may expect the further conclusion that the institutional setting most likely to encourage growth of man as man has many of the traits associated with the ideal of community.

Hegel described the community as existing on two levels, the family and the state. The family is a natural, unreflected-upon community. Each identifies with a larger whole, but the identification occurs largely at the level of feeling. The state exists as a more deliberate form of community. In patriotism the individual, recognizing that the state incorporates the conditions necessary for his own development, knowingly identifies with it and thus forms a corporate bond with his fellow citizens.

Much of the unpopularity of Hegel's political philosophy stems from the last-mentioned theme, and his development of it led him to some intolerable views, including a favourable attitude toward war. But the objections mainly concern his manner of applying a generally plausible idea. A strong case for community is made by describing it as a feature of the social setting called for by the idea that freeing the individual from repressive institutions that inhibit his full development requires growth of a human world that answers to his nature. What is implausible is the contention that the nation-state is the ultimate form of community.

In Hegel the conceptions of community and of ethical life are closely related. An ethical life (*Sittlichkeit*) is the result of a person's identifying with a wider sphere. Thus, being a member of a family may form an ethical life; and in a more adequate way the patriot who identifies with his state enjoys an ethical life. It isn't entirely clear how this idea of 'identifying with' something should be analysed, but certain features may be mentioned. Obviously, to identify with something else doesn't necessarily involve losing one's own separate identity. The experience of participants in the Czechoslovakian revolt of 1968 is to the point. Some who manned the clandestine radio services during the early period of Russian occupation said afterward that they had never felt more free than they did during that period of great personal danger.[6] Here were people who had wholly identified with a cause, and with fellow patriots who had the same cause, and yet were so far from losing themselves in that

6 J. Wechsberg, *Voices* (Garden City, N.Y., 1969).

identity that they felt totally energized and free. They emphatically sensed that they had found themselves in an ethical life.

Experiences of this sort are relevant to our estimate of the leisure-oriented society. In referring to an ethical life, Hegel appears to have had two aspects of the act of identifying with a larger whole in mind: first, through such identification a person may find a nearly total release of his own energies; second, only by doing so will his life qualify as ethical. In a quite ordinary sense of the term, one's life is not ethical if it is wholly given over to personal pursuits and goals. And perhaps it is our acceptance of this fact that contributes to the contrast in depth of personal involvement between pursuits we see as directed toward the well-being of a larger whole with which we identify and those we see as wholly self-referring.

The contrast between a work-oriented and a leisure-oriented society reproduces that between an ethical life and its opposite. A leisure-oriented life is directed toward producing benefits for the individual himself, his ease, his distraction, his growth. And the idea of a leisure-oriented society is that of a network of institutions appropriate to such a life. We may now say that it is the idea of a society that does not naturally elicit an ethical life. The effect of Hegel's outlook is to call into question the worthiness of the leisure ideal and its practicality, since in its own terms it has failed if it leaves the leisured individuals quite miserable. Perhaps a life of leisure, being largely devoted to oneself, is fated to be an unhappy one.

The challenge extends to Mill's principle of equal freedom as the principle for distribution of rights, and thereby to the idea of a private sphere. The principle of equal freedom contemplates a social world partitioned off into private spheres, from each of which the individual whose sphere it is may if he chooses exclude others on the basis that they have no rights to entry, and it contemplates a state whose main reason for being is to enable people to enforce these claims. Hegel, by contrast, applying the idea of an ethical life to the state at large, recognizes the importance of private spheres, but envisages their subordination to a nation state with which the citizens have identified and to which they sense a primary loyalty. This involves a shift of emphasis from people staking claims against one another, asserting rights over one another, to their claiming a right to a responsible place in the whole with which they identify: a right to a responsible, contributory station, and a right to carry out the duties associated with that station. The leisure-oriented society would eliminate so far as possible the conditions that make it intelligible to assert such a claim. On Hegel's view the focus of a person's life should not be assertion of rights over others to assure a spacious private domain in which to work out his own destiny; instead, it should be on a place he has in an admirable larger whole, in which he finds the conditions for his own growth while working to secure the well-being of that whole.

Although it is clear that Hegel rejects the utilitarian criterion for rightness, it is not clear what he would put in its place. By directing attention exclusively to the future, to outcomes of courses of action, the utilitarian (Mill) minimizes the importance of and weakens our feeling for the continuity of the past with the present. When this feeling for continuity is raised to the level of a principle, we have pure conservatism. But Hegel's conservatism was rather more subtle than that which claims that the traditional way of doing things is always the best way. The past is not something wholly other, to be set alongside our lives and world, but, he held, there is one course of development, an historic project, in which our ancestors, ourselves, and our descendants are all involved and which it is rational for us to continue. Once it is perceived that the 'customary way' does not refer to a static routine which because it has been endlessly repeated ought to persist but refers instead to an historic project, then the idea of conservatism and continuity with the past is seen as giving a novel role to the present, our own distinctive contribution to furtherance of the project. The role is discovered not by looking to the probable consequences of alternative courses of action, as the utilitarian would have it, but by looking to what man has been and done and, in a certain manner, extrapolating from that.

The bearing of these remarks on our attitude toward technology is uncertain. Thus, one may notice that the history of mankind is very much a history of technology, and that in large part man's historic project is that of perfecting a technology by which he makes nature over to suit his purposes. So far it would seem that Hegel's thought cannot be opposed to technology in spirit. But in addition technology disturbs tradition. Technology is a revolutionary force, and to humanize it would be to perfect this feature – to make tenable and livable the radically new futures technological competence puts within our grasp.

IV

We find in Mill a cluster of ideas sympathetic with the model of a leisure-oriented society, and in Hegel a conflicting cluster sympathetic with the model of a work-oriented society. On one side we have the ideas of making decisions by looking hard-headedly at the probable consequences for human life; of securing conditions that enhance individual growth and of the importance of non-coercive environments in which people have no alternative to making their own decisions; of a society in which people have extensive individual rights, and therefore occupy numerous private spheres from which they may exclude others; and of a government that principally exists to support such arrangements. On the other side we have stress on the indispensability of civilized and civilizing institutions for growth, so that in pursuing freedom it isn't sufficient to remove constraints but is necessary as well to await or create institutions that answer to our nature; on the role of community as a feature of those institutions; on the importance of ethical life for prompting energetic engagement of men in their world but also to assure that individual life is worthy; and on the value of continuity with the past and with nature, a continuity that is threatened by technology, however humanized.

We may suppose that most people will sense that both of these sets of ideas are plausible. Growth, individuality, writing off the past and focusing on the human quality of a future made possible by bringing to bear all of the technological skills available, are powerful themes. Alas, so also are continuity, human relatedness, and devotion to responsible projects in which the value of the individual and his life are embedded in larger contexts. And yet so profound is the chasm that divides the two clusters of ideas – as profound as that which divides the two models for the future they support – that we cannot simply merge them.

The key issue posed by their opposition concerns the appropriate relation of the individual with the social groupings and orders that form his world. One view of that relationship envisages individuals having and pressing rights against one another. It understands the problem of social justice as that of achieving a fair distribution and impartial enforcement of rights. And it advances a principle of equal freedom as the criterion of fairness. The domain in which a fair balance of rights is maintained is imagined to be inhabited by fully developed individuals, rejoicing in their individuality, and this development and spontaneity are seen as supported by the fact that the domain is ordered by a principle of equal freedom. Each finds the social world to be a means to his own personal development and satisfaction, subject to the constraint that he take no more of the benefits than are his due.

The critic of this view, however, has a different picture. The individuals may be free, within the sphere of their rights, and the distribution of rights fair, but their freedom is hollow. They are unable to enjoy their rights unless in addition they have power to do the things they are free to do. And this isn't assured. The freedom and rights are conceived, rather, to consist only in being permitted to act, which is something short of having capability of doing so. Actually to reach the envisaged result, a collection of fully developed individuals rejoicing in their individuality, requires, more than mere permissiveness, the presence of positive conditions – subjective and institutional – that bestow real capability of doing that which is formally permitted.

The opposing view of the appropriate relationship of the individual with the social groupings and orders that form his world is that to which the term 'ethical life' has been applied. Now, instead of pressing rights, but fairly, against the society, stress is on an active, co-operative relationship. The important feature of the social world is its enabling the person to play a useful, meaningful part within it. When the person himself takes this view, his life is turned outward. What dominates is not individual rights, but right. Social justice consists not in all having their fair share of the benefits and freedoms that the association offers its members, but rather in each having a socially meaningful station, through which his own needs are satisfied in activity that benefits the whole community. This second view gains its attractiveness from the fact that when the principle of justice it is based on is realized, people's lives are ethical. This means that they sense that their principal concerns are serious and that through the support the society lends to their pursuit of these concerns their personal dignity is acknowledged.

A critical view of the wholistic perspective, however, shows up a different face. The stress that the wholist places on the importance for ethical life of people having a fixed place or station calls into question his commitment to development of people's particular, distinctive capabilities. Typically, we find that he begins with a conception of what human nature is, and then tries to envisage a world in which people occupy stations that answer to that. This leads Plato to identify justice with everyone *staying* in the place he is fitted for. It leads Aristotle to an élitist view in which the many toil so that the few who alone possess a capability of fully developing the common human nature may have leisure in which to do so. It leads Hegel to associate being free with obeying laws that make obligatory the mode of life suggested by this common human nature. It leads lovers of community to favour the individual's identifying with spatially defined units – whether villages, neighbourhoods, or nation-states – and with an established mode of life to which he is to adapt.

As a result the distinctive traits of particular people are regarded as unimportant. The ideal of self-realization becomes that of fulfilling an imagined common human nature, not the actual capabilities of actual people. It is this fact that underlies the just complaint that wholists do not effectively acknowledge the value of individuality. Doing so would require giving up the emphasis on fixing the person to a static station and reaching the conception of a more open relationship of the person with his world.

CHAPTER SEVEN

Objectivity

The results of the preceding chapters may be summed up in the following propositions. First, we must finally accept the untenability of the value system by which we have ordered our lives for the past few hundred years. This value system, with its emphasis on material well-being and consumption, and its dedication to economic growth, has been subjected to criticism from many points of view. But regardless of our reaction to the criticism, it is an inescapable fact that even if we wanted it to the system cannot persist much longer. Exponential growth of population and environmental demand, depletion of resources, pollution, and, in consequence, interference with delicate but essential ecosystems responsible for many of the conditions for human life on the planet, make it likely that sometime during the lives of our children the system will simply collapse under the weight of the problems it has created.

Secondly, to respond adequately and in time we require a model of the kind of social order we desire to replace the one now dying. With this, responses to particular day-to-day problems may gain coherence from the fact that each is a further step toward the ideal the model depicts. Achieving such a model and the will to be guided by it are made difficult by the decadence of the system under which we live: preoccupation with private affairs keeps us from fully recognizing and responding to our plight. Most of us are latter-day Neros. But when the will to overcome decadence is found, and serious search for a model made, we are stymied by collective ambivalence. Our intellectual tradition points us toward two eminently attractive but diametrically opposed models. These may be seen as built up of opposing responses to three large issues: our estimate of technology, of community, and of the relative values of work and leisure. One, the work-oriented model, contemplates a world in which the focal values are those associated with humanized work, our commitment to technology is substantially withdrawn, and the local communities of the past, with their integrity and collective lifestyles, are restored or adapted to the changed conditions. The other, the leisure-oriented model, contemplates a world in which so far as possible machines do the work while men at their leisure freely pursue their own individual development and enjoyment, technology is humanized so that man is enabled to live with it, and the traditional community is superseded by individualistic patterns of social organization.

Thirdly, these opposed models express, in terms of contemporary issues and possibilities, two historic world-views, wholism and individualism. The former is objectified in village communities, distinguished by the wholeness of the collective lifestyle they exhibit, and their insularity; the latter is objectified in town life, most especially cities, and its essential feature is the pulverization of the wholeness of village life by opening up within the settlement numerous and extensive private spheres in which the inhabitants locate the primary values and meanings of their existence. These world-views receive explicit statement and support in philosophical systems. Individualism focuses on the prime value of fully developed individuality and defends evolution of private spheres as institutionalizing a domain of rights that contains the soil in which individuality may grow. Wholism focuses on the prime value of ethical life, in which the individual transcends himself by identifying with a larger whole with reference to which he finds the point of his individual existence. Ambivalence regarding the leisure- and work-oriented models stems from our sensing that, while the prime values focused on by individualism and wholism are both ultimate and have a place in any compelling model of the future, neither of the models provides that place. Leisure, individualized lifestyles, and a humanized technology are not consonant with ethical life; while work, community, and withdrawal of commitment to technology appear to jeopardize full, individual self-development.

II

The preceding six chapters point to the conclusion that our model of the future should be built around a mode of self-transcendence in which individuality is affirmed. We lack and need vision of a world in which ethical life and individuality support one another. Discussion of the environmental crisis, community, and work and leisure has suggested some of the ingredients of this vision. Responsibility, professionalism, and the original Greek concept of leisure, the three positive ideas to surface in that discussion, all refer to ways of relating with other persons and things that involve both self-transcendence and self-affirmation. Activity that is responsible, professional, or leisurely is essentially self-directed, and engages the person's energies and capabilities in fundamental ways. To the degree that autonomy and personal involvement are lacking, the activity is simply less responsible, less professional, less leisurely. But equally, such activity directs the person outward, toward other persons and objects to which value is attributed, and the self affirmed through the activity is one defined by its relationship with those persons and objects.

1 *Responsibility*

Through his activity a person inevitably relates with something beyond himself. Self-transcendence is an occasional feature of that relationship. A responsible person senses that his action sustains or creates value intrinsic to the natural environment. He does not act *on* the environment to satisfy a need, interest, or want - his own or someone else's - but he acts *for* it. Thus, he does not assert rights over others. In an elementary sense, the action is self-forgetful - of oneself as *interested*, a possessor of rights - and the relationship with the object is as a result open and responsive, not defensive. When the value attributed to nature is not in jeopardy, so that the action consists simply in beholding a natural scene and being enthralled, the value is sensed as *there*, and in his appreciation of it a person does not set it over against himself but gives himself up to it. In extreme cases, such as religious 'enthusiasm,' this may be experienced as the enveloping oneness of oneself with something beyond that is only vaguely comprehended. In ordinary aesthetic experience it consists in absorption in a concrete object vividly present. When the value ascribed to nature is in jeopardy, so that action to preserve or establish it is called for, this same continuity with the object may be realized. The opposition that the action involves does not separate the person from the object, but rather unites him with it over against the elements that put it in jeopardy.

The crucial distinction is that between asserting a right over others and acknowledging or pursuing a value ascribed to an object. Why this so critically influences the tone of our experience is suggested by a standard definition of 'personality' and a corresponding psychoanalytic definition of the 'ego.' In legal contexts, a person is a bearer of rights and duties, and it is common in moral theory to extend this idea by holding that the essential feature of 'moral personality' is possession of moral rights and duties. These definitions of personality rest on an underlying commonsense distinction between persons and things, according to which a thing is an entity that may fittingly be used by us in pursuit of our purposes, without our needing to ascribe purposes or ends to it that must be in turn be respected. A person, by contrast, is a being with ends that should be respected, a being not to be simply *used*. The idea of a legal right as it figures in the legal definition of a person is but the translation into a legal context of this concept of a being who ought not to be simply used, and the notion of moral personality is a similar translation into a moral context. To assert a right is to demand that one's ends be respected, that one not simply be used for the ends of others; it is to demand to be treated as a person. By recognizing an individual's rights, the law acknowledges that he is a person - or, if we care to think of it this way, it bestows personality on him.

A second feature of our understanding of a person is that being a person involves being intrinsically valuable. The best terms for expressing the kind of value this refers to are 'dignity' and 'worth.' This leads to the idea that a person has reality in his own right, is distinct, individual, other than everything else. The connection of the two features is that in asserting a right, thus claiming status as a person, we ascribe to ourselves ends that should be respected, which involves the claim that we have worth or dignity and exist as something distinct from and other than everything else.

As a result, a person whose stance in the world gives special prominence to his rights is led by this fact to a pronounced sense of his distinctness, of discontinuity between himself and the objects and persons his activity relates him with. A stance that relegates his own interests and wants to a subordinate status, and that orients the person, his attention, energies, and concerns toward objects, yields a markedly different awareness of self. The sense of otherness is replaced by one of continuity and relatedness. It goes without saying, of course, that a person's life situation may be such that he cannot or ought not lower his guard by minimizing his rights and adopting a primary orientation of responsibility toward objects. In particular, to ask a victim of social injustice to place any other concerns above his concern to have his rights acknowledged would be absurd, although we might admire him if he did so. And probably few people are so secure in their rights that it would be reasonable altogether to neglect them. But these admissions are compatible with the view that an anxious concern for one's rights is reprehensible, and that a more admirable conception of the human person is provided by the idea that he is defined by his manner of relating with and contributing to values beyond himself, not by the rights he holds over others or by the correlative duties he has in virtue of their rights over him.

The psychoanalytic theory that relates the ego with defence mechanisms points to a similar result. H.S. Sullivan held that a principal human concern is maintenance of self-esteem.[1] Threats to self-esteem activate mechanisms, paranoia for example, designed to preserve a person's satisfaction with himself. His self-estimate is enhanced if he can come to believe that his failures are not an outcome of personal limitations but are caused by persistent and malicious enemies. A person's concept of himself is a particular selection from and distortion of his various character traits. These he bundles up and presents to the world in the fond hope that by convincing others and through them himself that this is what he really is he will have an effective shield to interpose between

1 *The Collected Works* (New York, 1956), II, pp. 3-11. Sullivan himself preferred the term 'dynamism' to 'mechanism' because the latter 'suggests a Diesel engine.' Where here I speak of maintenance of self-esteem, Sullivan referred to personal security. In any case, the idea is that of 'states which are attendant upon being valued, respected, looked up to ... ' (p. 11).

himself and the world. By this stratagem he strives to protect his self-esteem against the battering it receives.

Although Sullivan may have overgeneralized there is obviously much truth in his view. But if we turn the theory around we get the result that if a person met no threats to his self-esteem he would have no sense of himself as something essentially distinct and apart from everything else. The effect of defence mechanisms is to vivify this sense. Regardless of whether we focus single-mindedly on threats to self-esteem or recognize other occasions that call forth defence mechanisms, the basic idea is that there are conditions of oneself to which one grasps. A stance in the world that is open, rather than defensive, not dominated by the idea that there is something precious in oneself that must be protected, but turned outward, toward objects in which value is seen or sought, is also a stance that does not activate an 'ego' and with it a pronounced sense of separateness from the objects one's activities implicate. Responsibility involves self-transcendence because it relates the person with his world in this open manner.

In an otherwise bad book, B.F. Skinner argues, correctly I think, that one of the required changes in the world of the future is relinquishment of the idea of personal dignity.[2] But he fails to understand both what this would involve and why it is desirable. The 'dignity' of the person is simply his status as a person, and he asserts his dignity by asserting his rights. His world makes this assertion possible by institutionalizing private spheres. A world in which personal dignity is a principal concern is one in which these spheres dominate and the public domain is subordinated to them. To find, as we have done, that this emphasis is not responsive to the three central issues created by rampant technology is to find that we must give up the idea of personal dignity as it has been understood over the past few centuries, and evolve patterns of social organization that relegate the complementary private spheres to a subordinate place. Thus, in his relations with the natural environment, a person's dignity rests on his ownership of land, on the conversion of nature into real property. He asserts his dignity by using and enjoying his property, by exercising his rights in it. The privacy of the property establishes his reality and distinctness as a person.

What happens when the relationship with the natural environment implied by this emphasis on one's rights is replaced by one in which a sense of responsibility vis-à-vis the natural environment is paramount? In this shift a person puts the idea of dignity to one side, as of lesser importance, and takes a stance by which instead of stressing his distinctness he stresses his continuity with what is beyond himself. Or, since 'dignity' is such an unqualifiedly honorific term, we may put it that he is led to reconceive the ideal so that he associates

2 *Beyond Freedom and Dignity* (New York, 1971), chap. 3.

his personal dignity with his capability of relating with the natural environment in a responsible manner; with his professional competence, by which he is enabled to carry on an admirable and valuable life pursuit; and with his capacity for leisure, by which he discovers the present and dwells there, actively savouring its immediacy. The practical counterpart of the shift in ideals is institutionalization of appropriate alternatives to the private spheres that complement personal dignity – establishment of the real possibility of functioning in the world in a responsible, professional, and leisurely manner.

To this point, I have been concerned with the sense in which responsibility involves self-transcendence. The other aspect is individual self-affirmation. Responsibility is self-imposed. Our acceptance of it is a personal decision reaffirmed on each occasion we act responsibly. Without that decision a person cannot be said to *be* responsible. Responsibility is thus not a casual feature of one's activity, but its appearance reflects an initiative taken by the responsible person, by which he defines, affirms, and asserts *himself*. But the self affirmed and asserted is not distinguished by an interest or want pursued by claiming rights over others; it is identifiable as a distinctive manner of contributing to values apprehended as lying beyond oneself. One's dignity then is grounded in the fact that one has the capability of making such a contribution. And institutionalization of channels by which the capability may find expression is public recognition and enforcement of the dignity of the person in this sense.

2 *Professionalism*

What has been said regarding responsibility is generally applicable to the ideal of professionalism, since the latter is responsibility showing itself in one's principal life activity. We may think of a professionalized occupation either as an alternative to work or as its perfection, and of a person's identification with professional colleagues and with the profession itself as an alternative to traditional community. The element of self-transcendence arises because a person's active dedication to his profession, his 'work,' implies that he is not primarily directed toward satisfaction of personal wants but toward adequate expression of the socially defined practice in his own professional performance. Ideally, a surgeon will value and be directed toward competent performance in the surgery and toward a higher level of health in the community; a teacher, toward activity in the classroom that satisfies the highest standards of the teaching profession and that contributes to informed students infected with a desire to learn. To the extent these motives are absent, neither the surgeon nor the teacher carries on his occupation as a profession; and to the extent people in other occupations, whether menial or grand, adopt this orientation they carry them on as professions. Doing so requires not merely a certain attitude on the part of those who carry on the occupation but also that the occupation itself be structured in an appropriate way.

While absorbed in and by the profession that occupies him, a person may nevertheless be totally engaged as an individual. Because autonomy is a defining trait of a professionalized occupation, success in the occupation is a personal challenge that activates distinctive traits and draws on highly individual resources. And dedication to the profession is a personal commitment in which the individual affirms himself. But, again, the self affirmed is defined by a distinctive manner of relating with matters beyond itself, not by features that separate it from everything else. It is nonsense to imagine that by becoming absorbed in something outside himself a person necessarily loses his identity, or that by being directed toward values that don't refer back to his own rights and private concerns he sacrifices or minimizes his individuality. Quite the reverse may well occur. Self-transcendence in which one affirms one's individuality can be an entirely prosaic affair, natural and familiar. Only, strangely, our theories about the appropriate ordering of human relations, by onesidedly emphasizing the self-interested person and the problem of adjusting his claims to the claims of others so that a fair distribution of rights will be achieved, or by emphasizing the reality and importance of the community per se, have made the coupling of transcendence with individuality seem unlikely, even paradoxical.[3]

3 Social contract theory is the form in which this stress on the self-interested person first found its way into Western political philosophy. The Hobbesian version of the theory holds in effect that our duty to obey the law (hence the authority of the state) arises from the fact that we or our ancestors mutually contracted to do so, or would have had we faced the option of doing so or existing in a 'state of nature'; that is, a condition in which our actions are not regulated by a coercive legal system. The Lockeian version makes actually having agreed (promised, contracted) paramount, and finds good reason for everyone agreeing in the fact that doing so is to the ultimate advantage of each. The best interpretation of Hobbes seems to be that the fact of agreeing is irrelevant, so that our reason for having and obeying a body of coercive laws is that despite the loss of freedom this entails the condition of each of us becomes considerably better, owing to the security we gain, than it would be in a state of nature.

Generally speaking, social contract theory was replaced, in the English-speaking world, by utilitarianism. Bentham and his colleagues and successors were committed to the view that pleasure is at once the only thing that is good in itself and the only thing that we deliberately pursue for its own sake – conversely, that pain is the only thing bad in itself and the only thing we deliberately avoid for its own sake. This coupling of a hedonistic theory of the good with a hedonistic theory of motivation gave utilitarianism its main character.

In legal theory, it led to the view that the objective of a legal system is to create an artificial identification of interests, in the following sense: a necessary condition of an action being criminal is that it introduces more pain than pleasure into the world (runs contrary to the interest of the community). But if the potential criminal finds that the crime he is contemplating is on balance pleasurable (is in his interest) he will in any case commit it. The problem of the law, then, is to devise a system of penalties for commission of criminal actions of such severity that, in light of the promised pain, the poten-

3 *Leisure*

In the original Greek sense to be at leisure is to dwell in the present. Of course, whatever one does or undergoes occurs in the present. But if there is contentment with what one is doing the successive steps involved in carrying it out may each be savoured. The passage from one to the next may seem to be not a matter of working toward a result that must finally be reached if the activity leading up to it is to have any significance; rather, it may seem to have its point and adequate reason for being at each step along the way. *Dwelling* in the present means finding that what the mind is directed toward at the moment – one's thoughts or imagined or presented sensuous material – is fine, good, satisfying, complete in itself. A person has no impulse to rush on to something else, but is content to linger with each moment and what it brings, and greets its successor and its contents with equal equanimity and enthusiasm.

tial criminal will no longer find it in his interest to do those things that run contrary to the interest of the community. By solving this problem a legal system would replace the natural incompatibility between the interest of the individual and that of the community by an artificial identification of the two. Since people will in any case 'pursue their own pleasure,' unless such an artificial identification of interests is created crime cannot be stopped.

In economic theory it led to, or provided a convenient underpinning for, the doctrine of the invisible hand. Here, people 'pursuing their own pleasure' gets translated into people seeking to maximize their personal wealth, on the assumption that the richer you are the happier you are. The theory asserted that if the social situation in which people seek to maximize their wealth is appropriate – which meant, roughly, free, competitive markets – then, reflexively, the 'wealth of the nation' would be maximized. That is, in such a situation a natural identification of the interest of the individual and that of the community would obtain.

In political theory it led to the idea that representative democracy with universal suffrage (as then understood) is the preferable political system. Such an arrangement plays in the political sphere the same role as that played in the economic sphere by free, competitive markets. Each will vote his interests, just as each will seek to maximize his wealth, so that a legislature will be formed in which the distribution of the interests of the representatives maps that of the electorate. These interests in turn will find expression in legislation that reflects the community interest. Thus representative democracy with universal suffrage would underlie a natural identification of the interests of the individual with that of the community.

The notions that 'everyone is self-interested' and 'everyone seeks his own pleasure' are notoriously ambiguous. In one sense they are vacuous: my interests are after all mine, whatever they may actually consist in, and in any case it is these I seek – if I'm truly interested. In another sense, these notions are neither vacuous nor, in general, true. Not everyone does seek 'his own pleasure' and no one seeks 'his own pleasure' all the time, in the sense that everyone, always, prefers just his own welfare or well-being (as he understands these) and cares not at all for the welfare or well-being of others whenever he thinks these run contrary to his own. Self-sacrifice does sometimes occur, and it is not less self-sacrificial because the person concerned prefers (has an interest in) the sacrifice. The two sides of the ambiguity involve the distinction between, respec-

Leisure, thus conceived, is the perfect form of self-transcendence in which individuality is affirmed. When we are at leisure, that toward which the mind is directed is experienced as continuous with ourselves. Music listened to at leisure is not sensed as something apart from us, but, as we say, we lose ourselves in the music. It is essential to the leisureliness of the experience that this should be so. So far as one does not dwell in the music it serves only as a background while the mind is otherwise occupied, or perhaps as a distraction. But, on the other hand, the 'loss of self' means only suspension of a different manner of relating with things outside ourselves, in which there is concern to get something *from* them – as when we assert a right – or to defend our self-esteem against imagined assaults. In suspending these modes of relationship with objects, we lose not ourself but our sense of our self as discrete, discontinuous. But we achieve a sense of a self that exists *in* relationship with the leisurely event. Dwelling in the present means dwelling in the music to which we attend in our leisure, but it is *we* who dwell in the music. Only, again, the self realized in this way is not one that distinguishes itself from everything else through its defensiveness or by asserting rights.

The experiences to which these remarks refer are perhaps sufficiently familiar. In the theory of art they are sometimes accounted for by the concept of psychic distance. It is said that the setting in which the play is presented, placing it within a proscenium arch with the audience to the front, looking on, assures that however absorbed he may be in the proceedings on stage, the spectator will not leap forward to save the heroine from the villain by paying the rent. There is 'psychic distance' between the audience and the play, despite the leisureliness of their experience of it and their absorption in its unfolding. The term 'psychic distance' doesn't explain anything, however, but merely gives a name to the fact that the spectator doesn't so far forget himself as to interfere with the action of the play. It is moreover a misnomer, since it sug-

tively, *whose* pleasure or interest it is and what *kinds of objects* one is interested in or that please one. Because all of our interests are, necessarily, *ours*, it does not follow that we are only interested *in* ourselves.

In the applications of utilitarianism to legal, political, and economic theory, it is clear that the appropriate sense of the hedonistic theory of motivation employed is that given by the second side of the ambiguity of 'self-interest' or 'own pleasure.' Similarly, that same sense must be understood when we find Hobbes grounding the authority of the law in the fact that it is in everyone's interest.

For Hobbes see *The Leviathan*, in any of numerous editions; for Locke, *Second Treatise of Civil Government*; for utilitarian legal theory, Bentham, *An Introduction to the Principles of Morals and Legislation*; for utilitarian economic theory, Adam Smith, *The Wealth of Nations*; for utilitarian political theory, James Mill, *An Essay on Government*. A useful survey of the entire utilitarian movement, organized along the lines indicated here, is found in E. Halévy, *The Growth of Philosophic Radicalism*, trans. M. Morris (Boston, 1955).

gests that the audience holds itself aloof, does not become wholly absorbed in the action. What is called 'psychic distance' is in fact the distancing of the play's world from the real world, coupled with the not surprising result that despite their absorption in the action the audience don't respond as they might to comparable action seen as occurring in the real world – by, for example, trying to pay the heroine's rent. One need not account for people's not jumping up on stage by supposing that their absorption in the action of the play is qualified in any way. It is rather that they are absorbed in a *play*, not in events outside the theatre, and react appropriately.

There is a sense then in which a spectator absorbed in a play may wholly forget himself. This means that he becomes for awhile unconscious of his own concerns outside the theatre. Since he dwells altogether in the present his experience is a prime example of leisure. But all the while he may be totally active – attentive, sensitive, reflective, and discriminating – and if empathic reactions are involved this activity may be muscular as well. The fact the experience is leisured doesn't necessitate that it be relaxing or that the individual be idle. If we had to imagine that he is sponged up by the action of the play, that he becomes absorbed in it as a passive spectator by merely placing himself before it and allowing it to work upon him, then we could not make out a significant sense in which he as an individual realizes and affirms himself in the event. His 'self-transcendence' in this case would be but an escape from himself. But when in his leisure a person is active, when his energies are brought into play in a fairly complete way, then the very fact that the experience is self-transcending gives it also a character of self-affirmation and realization. But the self affirmed and realized is a self directed toward and continuous with objects.

The distancing of the play's world from the real world is in effect a bracketing off of the time during which the play is performed from the past and future. As a result, the events on stage are not interpreted by reference to events in the world outside the theatre – what had been or will be – but are taken in their own terms, so that it becomes possible to establish the time and place of the *play's* action. By bracketing off the time of the play the actors structure the situation so that the audience dwell in the present. That is, psychic distance is simply the fact that the experience of the audience is leisured, referred to negatively.

III

Responsibility, professionalism, and leisure all involve the individual's being directed toward values beyond himself, and his development and realization of himself as a being who exists in relationship with those values – a being defined by traits that find expression in appreciating or sustaining the values we associate with the natural environment, the various ends toward which the professions are directed and the practice leading up to them, and the objects to which we attend in leisurely activity. The common thread running through these various manifestations of self-transcendence is *objectivity*. The ultimate basis for building a model for the future around the ideals of responsibility, professionalism, and leisure is that these are forms of objectivity, characteristic modes of an objective life.

Unfortunately, a use of the term 'objectivity' has crept into the language according to which to be objective is to be uncommitted, uninvolved, uninterested, aloof. Comparable connotations are sometimes associated with disinterestedness and impartiality. Acceptance of these connotations removes from our vocabulary any straightforward way of referring to one of the most important dispositions a human being can have. Roughly speaking, objectivity, impartiality, and disinterestedness are synonyms. None implies lack of interest or concern, but they all refer to the character of one's commitment. To be objective is to be committed in a way that takes adequate account of all the relevant factors. To resolve an issue objectively or disinterestedly is to set aside one's biases and special interests and be influenced only by the facts, interests, and beliefs that are relevant to the issue. It is to decide the matter on its merits. Objectivity as a trait of character is a standing disposition to react that way. Every person exhibits the disposition in some degree, but no one exhibits it consistently or totally.

When we are in doubt about a practical matter and wonder what 'ought' to be done, we may have in mind any one of at least three different kinds of concern. (1) We may be uncertain as to the course most likely to satisfy some interest of ours: Ought I to travel by the back road or the expressway during the rush hour (which route will get me there faster)? (2) At the other extreme, we may be in doubt as to what, all things considered, is the moral course of action. This latter concern may be expressed by putting the question: What ought *one* to do? To put it this way is to ask, in effect, what an objective person would do. It is to inquire as to the course of action indicated by the merits of the case. In putting the moral question we attempt to set biases and special interests to one side and settle the matter disinterestedly. (3) Finally, sometimes when we wonder what we ought to do we think we know the course that is in our interest, and the course a disinterested person would choose, but are undecided between the two courses, whether to be prudent or moral. The ultimateness of the idea of objectivity is indicated by the fact that if a person voices this indecision openly in the form 'What ought one to do?' the only possible answer is that he ought to be objective, that is, choose the course an objective, disinterested person would choose – since this is only to say that he ought to do what he ought to do. The ultimateness of the moral, objective point of view, and therefore of a model of society that expresses such a point of view, is that this is the one that all things considered a person or a people *ought* to adopt.[4]

Responsibility, professionalism, and leisure are modes of objectivity or standing attitudes that find their appropriate expression in disinterested action, owing to the way each turns a person toward the objects and persons he confronts. His relationship with the world is receptive. The values are seen as there and he turns toward them so as not to shield some from the rest, or to distinguish mine from thine. Responsibility, professionalism, and leisure involve an open stance inconsistent with the personal bias that follows on centring on one's own wants and interests and with the incipient fanaticism that is a ground condition of the lives of those who have strong identifications with groups defined by their differences from other groups, religious, civic, or national.

There are two additional reasons for regarding responsibility, professionalism, and leisure as modes of objectivity. First, ideally, each involves a stance that is not merely open but affective. A responsible person *cares* about and for the natural environment. A professional is *committed* to the occupation with which he identifies. In leisure one is *absorbed* by and *alive* in the present moment. And in each case this affective component is not incidental but essential. Care, commitment, and lively absorption do not assure responsibility, professionalism, and leisure, but the latter are impossible without them: a careless person is irresponsible, an uncommitted person unprofessional, and one incapable of becoming absorbed in the present cannot know leisure. What above all consolidates objectivity is affection for the subject-matter concerning which objectivity is wanted. A father who loves his children has the strongest possible motive for treating them all fairly. A scholar devoted to his subject is similarly impelled toward gaining an unbiased comprehension of it. Affection works against objectivity, love against justice, only when it is exclusive or partial. When open, contemplating no closure, it transforms objectivity, considered as a formal character of a person's action, into a standing disposition.

Second, objectivity involves a relationship with the world that is non-exploitative. The stance is one of allowing the facts and values that are elements of the situation one confronts to be felt and to have their weight, rather than to

4 This association of the 'moral ought' with objectivity is elaborated and defended at length in two papers of mine: 'The Justification of Morality,' in *Studies in Philosophy and in the History of Science*, ed. R. Tursman (Lawrence, Kansas, 1970), pp. 18-29; and 'Utility and Rights,' in *Concepts in Social and Political Philosophy*, ed. R.E. Flathman (New York, 1973), pp. 468-84. The view is of the same type as and, I think, not necessarily inconsistent with, those that associate being moral with being rational, and that identify the 'moral point of view' with that of a disinterested observer.

force them into a mould, to impose one's own demands on them. Exploitation is thus seen as a result of coupling two attitudes in our action upon an object: first, the attitude that the object is but a means for the satisfaction of some need or want either of ours or of some group on whose behalf we act; second, the attitude that our action is an attempt to impose on the object a form or result that we have conceived and for which it is but raw material. Avoidance of these manners of dealing with objects, in non-exploitative action, involves apprehending the object as itself valuable or potentially valuable, so that our efforts are on its behalf – in acting on it we are doing something not for ourselves but for it or for the whole we and it form. In addition, non-exploitative action involves the view that if the objective sought is reached this success is not to be understood as our having stamped a desired form on possibly recalcitrant material, but rather results from our having influenced a process that had a capability of working out in the way it did, so that our action was essentially a manner of contributing to and co-operating with that process in the interest of improving the chances of success.

Responsibility, professionalism, and leisure all involve this non-exploitative stance, each in relationship with a different subject-matter. When the natural environment is dealt with responsibly, we place ourselves in its orbit, deferring to its exigencies. In the ecological perspective, this is exemplified in the attitude that natural things form ecosystems with self-maintaining tendencies we are to respect. And when the passivity of this perspective is corrected by accepting the creative role of men within ecosystems, their contribution if responsible remains non-exploitative owing to the fact that it is an attempt to enhance values attributed to the natural domain and this by eliciting release of potentialities intrinsic to it.

Professionalism is similarly non-exploitative in that the professional competence is a skill enabling one to co-operate with processes beyond oneself in order to initiate a development that will end in the desired result. Thus, a doctor doesn't cure his patient and the teacher doesn't educate the child. Rather, each makes a distinctive and necessary contribution to a process, to which many other factors are contributed, including not least contributions by the patient and student, that are calculated to enable the process to develop toward a cured patient and an enlightened, inspired student. This non-exploitative perspective is exhibited when a physician does not react to loss of a patient by blaming himself for not having saved him, but focuses instead on what there was, if anything, that he might have done but failed to do – which leaves open what is obvious in itself, that the situation may have been beyond his control and, in general, that neither success nor failure is wholly his own doing, not a result he imposes.

The non-exploitative aspect of leisure is shown by the totality with which the leisured person enters the object he attends to and follows its lead. It is not grasped as something to be moulded, worked upon and over, but is taken and sought out for what it may be. And in those leisurely activities that involve 'making,' nevertheless it is a feature of their leisureliness that the making is a drawing out from the material at hand of an object that seems the appropriate development of the material. The mood or atmosphere of the day finds *its* voice in the poem, and the poet consulting his muse, or like an Aeolian harp bending with the wind, is in the same relationship with his material as is the Socratic philosopher, a midwife who does not create but merely draws forth what was conceived elsewhere.

IV

What is at issue here is the relationship of the person and of the race itself with its objects. And since it is in this relationship that a person defines himself we may also say that what is at issue is our concept of ourself, and, more broadly, of the race. In one sense the idea that we are to build our model of the future around a mode of self-transcendence in which individuality is affirmed will gain ready assent, given the association of this with objectivity. But in another sense the position is highly radical. How radical, and how great the social transformation we would be led to if we took it seriously, may be seen by considering our underlying understanding of what it is to be human. It is, I suppose, inevitable that, when looking to prehistory we survey the broad sweep of events associated with 'the emergence of man,' we sense that we are looking back on a process that differs not in detail but fundamentally from the emergence of any other species. The emergence of any species means its development of traits that distinguish it from other species, so that it has a character peculiar to itself. But we imagine that the developed defining traits of man mark him off from other species in a distinctive way. I doubt that anyone, no matter how naturalistic his orientation, fails to sense that the species man is a very special case among the species of living things. Answers usually given to the question 'What is Man?' don't account for this imputation of uniqueness. Thus, man is said to be the *rational* animal; more prosaically, the featherless biped; the tool-making animal; the only creature who knows he will die; or the only one who seeks to define himself. These are all differences to be sure, but not differences that account for the sense that man is radically distinct from other species. Although each of the answers suggested is roughly true, none satisfies. If we draw our answer out of a survey of the actual steps in prehistory by which man emerged as a radically distinct species, rather than statically by searching about for traits common and peculiar to members of the emerged species, we are more likely to focus on matters that make the question 'What is it to be man?' so poignant.

The human race is an object with a career owing to the continuity of individual members of the race with one another. Each is born of parents from whom he inherits a genetic make-up continuous with that which their parents passed on to them. As a result our ancestors live in and through ourselves. And each is born into a social world articulated into institutions that reach back with what from some points of view are trivial modifications to the earliest days of the race's career. We ourselves sustain the continuity of the race by transmitting the genetic inheritance and vivifying the institutions through which the potentialities established by the inheritance develop. The implication of these facts is that when we piece together the main steps by which man emerged it is *our* beginnings, not those of some others like ourselves, that we comprehend.

Man's man-like ancestors from their first appearance over twenty million years ago were probably tool-users. An important aspect of the intervening period is the increasing sophistication of their tool-kits. Although the very fact of tool-use involves severance of continuity between the user and the object on which it is used, initially this established no notable distinction between man and the other primates. Chimpanzees using sticks to coax ants from their nests perform an action comparable to that of an ant-eater using his tongue for the same purpose. Similarly, there is no profound difference between a lion's tearing the flesh of its prey with its teeth and early man's use of a crude scraper. Tools are, in the first instance, extensions of anatomical equipment and are put to the same uses, satisfaction of vital needs of the users. So far, given a setting in which some creatures satisfy their needs with superior anatomical equipment and one makes up for anatomical deficiencies with tools – sharpened sticks rather than sharp claws to make the kill, fire rather than a roar to stampede game, scrapers rather than teeth to remove flesh – the human tool-users are not significantly different from the rest.

Tool-making is, of course, a more momentous facility than tool-use, for when this is generalized as a capacity to fashion tools to suit a wide range of purposes it gives a flexibility no imaginable stock of anatomical equipment could match. The result for man was a significant quantitative difference between his capability of satisfying his needs and the other species' capability of doing so. As this increased capability develops it does not so much lead to increasing levels of satisfaction of the same needs – more food or more time to rest between hunting forays – as it does to more elaborate needs and more refined institutions to facilitate attempts to satisfy them. Thus, early man's shift to big game hunting brought a need for close co-operation over long periods of time that finally established itself as the family, an institution that in turn spawned needs. And sympathy, the fundamental human relationship that made such co-operation possible, would appear to be the source of concern for the dead, which is reflected in the practice of burial. Archaeological evidence of burials more than a hundred thousand years ago suggests that by that time man had evolved the rudiments of religion, thus opening up another domain of previously unfelt needs.

As new needs appear, and institutions for organizing his efforts to satisfy them are established, man gradually constructs and elaborates a *human* world. What we call the emergence of man is at bottom the emergence of this world and of its dominance over the natural realm within which it is placed and with which it was initially continuous. At the base of this world within a world is a set of practices, generally followed and 'authoritative' ways of doing the things that it occurs to humans to do. Tacitly, if not explicitly, these practices are understood in certain ways, so that those who follow them attribute value to their activities and thus create a reason-for-being of their life as a whole. The 'human world' is this system of practices (as understood by the participants) plus the tool-kit by which the practices are carried on, the physical setting and equipment.

Just as the emergence of man is emergence of the human world, so his distinctness is the distinctness of that world from the natural domain other living species inhabit. No other animal separates himself from nature in the way implied by our creation of a human world. We experience how deep-rooted is the association of our conception of ourselves with this distinctness when we are told that man's original habitat was the African savanna and that the original focal point of his existence was the watering-hole to which, each evening, bands of the various species of animals who inhabited the savanna would come and quietly await their turn to approach the water, all the while apprehensively casting their eyes around for signs of danger. Seeing our ancestors – ourselves – in that setting, in that relationship with the rest of nature, has a strange impact on us. Although one might have imagined that contemplation of the scene would call forth a sense of an earlier, now lost, integrity of human life with its natural surroundings and with other living things, instead we are bound, I think, to apprehend these early humans as estranged, as still wandering, not yet having found their home. We sense that their proper habitat is not the savanna but the *human* world, a domain that either excludes nature or transforms it into an 'environment,' and that they are not at home in the world until their work of constructing this domain is well underway.

The sense, then, that man is something special among the animals, not a species among species, with his own distinguishing traits, but a species set over against all the other species, is an apt response to the fact that by erecting a world within and against the natural world he has *created* a special status for himself. But if in this way he has made it inevitable that he will perceive the distinction between himself and everything that is *not*-man to be quite fundamental, it is not inevitable that he will adopt any particular view of the nature of that distinctness – or, what comes to the same thing, of the nature of his relationship with that which he senses to be radically other than himself.

Robert Redfield has identified three views men have taken at one time or another of their distinctive relationship with 'not-man': ' ... to maintain it, to obey it, or to act upon it.' The first he finds among the Zuni, for whom, according to Ruth Bunzel, the critical feature of man's relationship with the world he confronts is an obligation to conserve its underlying order: 'The attitude is one of doing one's part in a persistent system.' The second he finds among the ancient Mesopotamians, for whom the central idea was that of obedience to more or less arbitrary divine commands. And the third is suggested by Daniel Boorstin's account of Thomas Jefferson's world-view, according to which, as Redfield describes it, man's obligation is 'to carry out, by changing nature and building institutions, the divine plan so providentially set out by God to be the American's happy destiny in the new continent.'[5]

When we place the views man has taken of his relationship with 'not-man' in an historical sequence they are seen to increasingly stress the distinctness of man and the subordination and fitness for exploitation of his 'other.' The three principal views of the relationship may be distinguished by the character of man's principal habitat at the time. First, as indicated, the habitat is the savanna. The second and third are those associated with the neolithic and urban revolutions, invention of food production and of cities. With passage from food gathering to food production man was enabled to pass from nomadic to settled life, and the habitat he settled into was the primitive village. Shortly thereafter he found the secret of growth and thus diversified and expanded his settlements until they formed the very different habitat that, in its most developed form, we experience in the modern metropolis.

In these three habitats, the savanna, the primitive village, and the city, man adopts three corresponding stances in relation with 'not-man.' On the savanna there was no imputation of dominance and radical otherness. Not having begun his work of constructing a human world, man related with his surroundings in a manner not fundamentally different than that shown by the savanna's other inhabitants. He had his distinctive vital needs, distinctive manners of pursuing them, and distinctive enemies. But these were all such as to consolidate his continuity with the habitat, his place within it and among its other inhabitants. We cannot reasonably suppose that he had a concept of this continuity, but he must have had a lifestyle that exhibited it. And since he was at least a percep-

5 *The Primitive World and Its Transformations* (Ithaca, N.Y., 1953), pp. 99-100.

tive creature we may imagine that the lived continuity was reflected in a dim awareness of his situation.

Associated with the tribal village as a habitat was a view of man's relationship with 'not-man' that Redfield regards as a central feature of the primitive world-view: ' ... the quality of the attitude toward the Not-Man is one of mutuality ... The obligation felt is to do what falls to one in maintaining a whole of which man is part.' Redfield illustrates the generalization by quoting an account of the Hopi attitude toward farm work: 'The Hopi ... working on the land, does not set himself in opposition to it. He works *with* the elements, not *against* them ... He is in harmony with the elements, not in conflict; and he does not set out to conquer an opponent. He depends on the corn, but this is part of a mutual interdependence; it is not exploitation.'[6]

Continuity on the savanna became mutuality in the primitive village. Man now had a world, hence an 'other,' but one with which he co-operated and for the condition of which he felt an obligation. The distinctive feature of the city as a habitat is that obligation in this sense and 'mutuality' are replaced by the view that whatever is other than man is an object to be used, a utility. On the one side there are human persons with their needs; on the other, things perceived as material for satisfying their needs.[7] Unless this distinction is made it is impossible to understand, and unless it is endorsed as correct it is impossible to accept, present-day humanism.

V

The work-oriented model of the future society is fundamentally sympathetic with the primitive view of man's relationship with 'not-man' and with basic features of the habitat appropriate to that view. It would not be fair to say that the model contemplates a return to the primitive lifestyle. Rather it seeks

6 *Ibid.*, pp. 105-6.

7 It is especially Kant who enforced this rigid distinction between 'persons' and 'things,' a position made inevitable by his manner of distinguishing between the noumenal and phenomenal realms. But the classic statement of the view of nature that the person/thing distinction involves is Locke's: 'God, who hath given the World to Men in common, hath also given them reason to make use of it to the best advantage of life and convenience. The Earth, and all that is therein, is given to Men for the Support and Comfort of their being.' *Two Treatises of Government* (London, 1690), pp. 244-5.

Not surprisingly, in view of his Kantian bias, John Rawls continues the theme in an excellent and much-heralded work in ethics and political philosophy, *A Theory of Justice* (Cambridge, Mass., 1972). Because he regards justice as the 'first virtue' of a society, and argues that the correct principles of justice to use are those that would be unanimously assented to by appropriately situated persons who consulted *only* their own self-interest (and that of their offspring), he is led to idealize a society in which, in the interest of justice, everything other than man (creatures capable of a sense of justice) is adjusted with an eye to securing a maximum, fair distribution of basic goods.

a contemporary adaptation of its essential features. Similarly, the leisure-oriented model is based on acceptance of the view of man's relationship with 'not-man' that finds its appropriate habitat in the city and seeks an adaptation that is sensitive to environmental issues and to the critique of the economics of growth.

Reasons have been found for seeking replacement of these orientations – continuity, mutuality, and exploitation – by one to which the general term 'objectivity' may be given, and which is exemplified in an attitude toward nature characterized by 'responsibility,' in a 'professional' attitude toward one's work, and in a 'leisurely' attitude toward the present and future. Objectivity has features that suggest each of the three earlier orientations, but is nevertheless unique. There is a sense in which the objective person is selfless, and through his selflessness a relationship of *continuity* with what is beyond him is established. Also, an objective person acknowledges that in his activity he is not so much producing results as co-operating with processes that originate elsewhere, so that he contributes to the outcome by entering into a relationship of *mutuality* with those outside processes. And, finally, an objective person acknowledges that there are values which are in jeopardy, that he has a responsibility to do what he can to preserve them, and that for this purpose it is necessary to *exploit* material at hand. But this exploitation is carried out in the interest of heightening the quality of a whole that is unlimited. Since this whole is seen as incorporating nature along with man, the person/thing distinction is transcended and the humanism and utilitarianism of recent centuries abandoned. Objectivity thus involves reversing the historic project of elaborating a human world that isolates man from nature and subordinates nature to his uses. But it reverses the project not by relinquishing power to make changes and accepting a passive role within nature but by taking a creative role within and on behalf of nature.

We have now to see some of the main features of the habitat appropriate to such a view of man.

CHAPTER EIGHT

A professionalized society

Five thousand million years ago nature created Earth. One thousand million years ago life appeared on it. Two million years ago man appeared as a distinct species, the erect primate. Life is continuous with the inanimate, man with the species from which he evolved, and each man with his ancestors, back to the original bands of homo erectus who waited their turn at the watering holes on the savannas of Africa.

As he has developed during the past two million years, man has increasingly taken the view that Earth, its natural features and the other kinds of life it contains, are there for his use. He has taken the view that they are *his* and has established a set of practices by which he systematically rearranges things on the planet to suit his own needs and preferences. Now it is clear that there are definite limits to the extent to which the planet can be manipulated for human use, to the point where a date can be given to the time when, at present rates of manipulation, the limits shall have been reached. The response on all sides is a call for greater prudence. If we are doing ourselves in by exploiting the environment, then we must learn to go at it more carefully, with an eye to the consequences. These are scarce resources that we as good economists must allocate wisely.

The continuity of each man with man, of man with other living species, and of life with nature are simply facts. Such continuities imply no particular valuation of the different ways the continuous elements interact with one another. The tacit understanding held by most in the West that the world *is* a human world, is *ours*, and the corresponding aspiration, when 'human' is taken as an ideal, to have Earth *become* a human world, are not shown to be literally false by the fact of man's continuity with nature.

It is possible, however, to describe an outlook and set of practices that would be favoured by anyone who wanted his life to be responsive to the fact of continuity, who wanted not to view Earth as an essentially human place and not to find that as a price of living on it at all he must adopt a stance toward it that he finds intolerable. Earlier chapters have shown, I hope, some of the ways in which a person might be led to this point, and have indicated as well some of the leading ideas on the basis of which he might attempt to go beyond it. These leading ideas are objectivity and its exemplification in professionalism, leisureliness, and responsibility. In the remaining chapters I shall develop these themes in a speculative way, sketching in some of the features of the outlook and set of practices they suggest. I shall not attempt anything approaching a detailed 'model of the future' to set over against the leisure-oriented and work-oriented models - that would be a large task that I am incapable of seeing through. The model I shall be working toward is that of an *Objective Society*. My principal concerns will be to identify its focal value and to contrast that with the focal values of the work- and leisure-oriented societies.

II

The feature of chief interest in any society is its focal value. By experiencing this value, members of the society experience as well the significance and final point of their life together. In preceding chapters I have mentioned four different opinions regarding the appropriate focal value for a society to have: contemplation, consumption, leisure, and work. An Objective Society is distinguished by its focusing instead on leisured performance of professional activity. This suggests two familiar principles that give direction to anyone practically committed to the ideal of an Objective Society: first, every person should have an opportunity to develop a distinctive talent or competence by which he might make a valuable contribution; second, there should exist in the society established channels through which those talents may find expression, and those channels should be open to anyone who possesses the appropriate developed talent. The resulting activity is professional in virtue of the manner in which the channels are structured.

In what ways do these principles distinguish a profession-oriented society from one that is work-oriented? 'Work' suggests a set of tasks a person *confronts* and for the performance of which he is paid. Their performance, or the result of their performance (depending on whether the work produces a service or a commodity), is desired by others who pay for it, sometimes directly but typically through a third party who mediates the relation between the producer and consumer. The idea of making work more humane is that of setting up the tasks so that they are more interesting to and rewarding for the workers.

Replacing work by professional activity involves eliminating most of these features. Instead of a set of tasks one confronts, the activity is *self*-defined. Rather than being paid *for* the activity, the person is, if necessary, subsidized *in order that* he might carry it out. The result of the activity may be a service or commodity, but need not be, and in any case the activity is not carried on simply in order that someone else may benefit but because it is seen as a worthy thing to do, in itself and in its results. Finally, in establishing opportunities for professional activity the ultimately guiding idea should not be to make the activity interesting and rewarding to the persons involved, nor to shape it so that it satisfies consumers; rather, the form of the activity should be fixed by *its* characteristics and requirements. It will be interesting and rewarding to the people who practise it because they are especially responsive to its values and are peculiarly qualified for carrying it on well. And those who enjoy or otherwise benefit from the activity will do so because of its quality, not because it is artfully contrived for their satisfaction.

In sum, a society in which professional activity is the focal value would not be one in which the key relationships and transactions are essentially commercial ones. We are not to think of the professional as producing a commodity, or of those who benefit in some way from his activity as consumers. Each of the contrasts mentioned results from replacing that image by one that locates value in the activity and its immediate object. The activity keeps its integrity by being guided toward that object, and by not being bent either in order that the person carrying it on may profit in some way or so that those who subsequently benefit from its results may get an extra thrill.

Imagine, for example, a film-maker who has a conception of the kind of film he wants to make and of how to make it. There are at least two ways he might go wrong. He might decide that the actors should enjoy themselves while working together on his film and make a different film than he otherwise would have in order that they might do so. What we want to say to him is that if the conception of the film had been right, and the actors right for it, then they could not have enjoyed making it unless it had been shot in the way its conception required. Similarly with work. If the job has to be altered to make it more interesting it probably wasn't worth doing in the first place. The solution doesn't lie in hoking it up so the workers will enjoy it anyway, but in reconceiving it so that it is fit to be enjoyed. Then the enjoyment will come as a natural accompaniment of respect for its worth and integrity. The second way the film-maker might go wrong is by slanting his film toward the audience in gratuitous ways – by inserting a tug at patriotic emotions here and exacting a big laugh there. These appeals to the audience are objectionable in themselves. But if the entire film were one continuous and coherent appeal to the audience's emotions it would be less gratuitous but an even worse film. We ask that it spring from an admirable conception and be finely wrought. Our appreciation (if it is evoked) should stem from our perception of *its* qualities. When instead the film-maker systematically caters to his audience the result is a feature-length commercial.

One word that fits here is 'uncompromising.' The person has a sense of how something should be done and goes to great lengths to get it right. The conceived requirements of the activity and of its object, not the needs of the actor, or even of the audience, dominate. If the object being made is a utility, the needs of the ultimate user should affect its conception. These needs are translated into a set of requirements for the object itself, and the activity proceeds by focusing altogether on those – the task of creating an object that meets, even exceeds, them. The art of cooking, for example, is based on features of the digestive tract and palate. But, in light of requirements that these make understandable, the serious chef tries to create an *object*. If he succeeds the diners don't just have pleasant or unpleasant sensations but are presented with a dish that is itself admirable. Their pleasure is not his *objective*, but is important when it confirms that he has done well. Consider, though, his reaction when people with no taste appreciate a poorly prepared dish.

When a person whose activity is directed toward production of objects he values, and whose dominating effort is to shape those objects in ways that satisfy his conception of how they ought to be shaped, is paid for his 'work,' this payment has a special significance that deserves to be identified. Ordinarily, we say he is paid for what he does. That is, he does it, he is paid, and if he weren't involved in doing it the money wouldn't come in. But the significance to him of his income is that it permits him to continue to make objects of that kind. The payment then is in the nature of a subsidy. It might be clearer to say, after the fact, not that he was paid for having done what he does but that he was paid in order that he might continue to do what he does. The conception of an Objective Society is fundamentally that of one in which this is true. A person has dignity in such a society because his life focuses on production of valuable objects he is especially competent to produce, a fact that is publicly recognized by his being subsidized to produce them. If someone is paid *for* what he does, a valuation is placed on the activity, or on its results, and the amount of the payment reflects the valuation. It answers the question 'How much is the work worth?'

When a person identifies with his work, it is natural for him to associate his worth with the valuation placed on it. He may thus have a good reason for not identifying with it since he ought to regard the accidental valuation others place on what he does as irrelevant to his worth as a person. But since at present work is the standard manner of finding a place in the social world, not to identify with it is to alienate oneself. The dilemma is overcome by shifting from work to professionalism, from the practice of paying people for what they do to one of paying them in order that they may do what they do, subsidizing them. The payment then wouldn't reflect a valuation of the activity, but an estimate of what is needed in order to continue it. This is to say that in an ideal state of affairs, where everyone has an opportunity to develop his talents and then to express them in activity that is worthy per se, people would in effect be on expense accounts.

At present, typically, a person's income is regarded as having been *earned* through his work. The principle involved is that the effort or skill the worker shows creates a rightful claim on the income he receives. In large part, our idea of justice is that of people getting what they deserve, and we suppose that one's income is deserved, if at all, to the degree he has worked for it. The assumption is shared by apologists for the system and its critics. Thus, Marx objects to capitalism on the basis that profit is possible only by short-changing the worker, that is, by paying him less than he deserves as measured by the amount of his work. This is to charge that capitalism is inherently unjust. To think of a person's income as a subsidy to permit him to carry on his occupation, rather than as a reward for having done so, is to give up the assumption regarding desert on which the argument depends. The assumption makes sense in circumstances where work is painful, so that since it lacks its own reason for being some extrinsic reason must be found. In these circumstances one *needs* a reward to justify the expenditure of effort involved. Work, then, exists as a means, unpleasant in itself but useful in view of the results of enduring it. When work is professionalized, the circumstances that make it sensible to construe income as an earned reward for having worked are eliminated. For then the person perceives his occupation as making sense in itself, its own reward, and what is wanted is not a pay-off but the means of carrying it on.

The two-mentioned features of the current arrangement, that by and large work exists as a generally painful type of activity that needs a pay-off to be justified, and that wages or other forms of income are justified, if at all, as earned and therefore deserved through work, go hand in hand. The fact that income is not only thought about but institutionalized in this way tends to consolidate work as generally a means to other ends rather than a mode of activity that has its point in itself. And the fact that it isn't seen as having its point in itself, and indeed is typically organized in ways that would make it absurd to pretend that it had, makes it sensible to institutionalize a wages system according to which income exists as a pay-off for having done something that one would rather have avoided doing. Accordingly, the idea of professionalizing the activities that currently exist as work cuts both ways: it directs us to transform income into a subsidy, and also to transform work so that it does acquire intrinsic significance, that is, to professionalize it.

III

The foregoing suggests Marx's slogan 'From each according to his ability, to each according to his need.' The prepositions 'from' and 'to' are inappropriate, as suggesting giving and receiving, as if what one received were a payment for

having made a contribution and the idea only were to tie the amount paid to need rather than to the value either of the product or of the work itself. And juxtaposing the two parts of the slogan suggests that receiving anything at all is conditioned by having given: one is to receive according to need, *provided that* he has given according to ability. So far, the slogan treats income as a reward, and thus envisages applying an underlying capitalist conception to a post-capitalist situation.

A second contrast with Marx results from his objections to the division of labour. Marx was impressed by the way, in mid-nineteenth-century Europe, people were sucked into narrow tasks and had their entire being and lives confined and clouded by that fact. He stressed two features of the division of labour. First, that a person caught up in a narrow occupation was likely to be stunted, since sinking all his energy into the task would leave him little opportunity to develop and express other facets of his nature. Second, that typically a person was stuck in his particular line of work for life: once having got into it its narrowing effect would make him increasingly unfit for anything else. The problem was both that the work was narrow and that the worker was, practically speaking, condemned to that particular narrowness throughout his life. Marx's solution, in looking forward to a more ideal state of affairs in a post-capitalist era, was to envisage a society of amateurs:

For as soon as labor is distributed, each person has a particular, exclusive area of activity which is imposed on him and from which he cannot escape. He is a hunter, a fisherman, a herdsman, or a critical critic, and he must remain so if he does not want to lose his means of livelihood. In communist society, however, where nobody has an exclusive area of activity and each can train himself in any branch he wishes, society regulates the general production, making it possible for me to do one thing today and another tomorrow, to hunt in the morning, fish in the afternoon, breed cattle in the evening, criticize after dinner, just as I like, without ever becoming a hunter, a fisherman, a herdsman, or a critic.[1]

1 *The German Ideology*, in *Writings of the Young Marx on Philosophy and Society*, ed. and trans. L. Easton and K. Guddat (Garden City, N.Y., 1967), pp. 424-5. It will be noted that the following interpretation of Marx is based entirely on this passage. A fuller account would require consideration of numerous other texts, including especially the 1844 *Manuscripts, Grundrisse, Capital*, and *Critique of the Gotha Programme*. S. Avineri treats the subject rather thoroughly in *The Social and Political Thought of Karl Marx* (Cambridge, 1970), especially in chaps. 4 and 8. Avineri's interpretation, based on all the available texts, is in line with my own. Basically, the upshot is that Marx's ideal is that of a work-oriented society of amateurs. It must be confessed that Avineri has difficulty reconciling his reading with some sections of *Grundrisse* (perversely, he makes no reference to this work in his discussion of 'The New Society,' chap. 8) and with the

One view of this is to suppose that Marx was idealizing a leisure-oriented society: people would be in a position to do and cease doing as they wished, without having to take account of the ways other people depend on them. And there is much evidence that he saw the possibilities of automation and looked forward to a time when, for the most part, men would be freed from the necessity to work. Unfortunately, this interpretation is difficult to reconcile with Marx's principle that everyone is to contribute according to his ability. Since a leisure-oriented society is one that has got past the point of needing to depend on people's contributions to it, it would make no sense to establish 'from each according to his ability' as its dominant motto.

A more plausible interpretation is to suppose that the activities he refers to – hunting, fishing, breeding cattle, and criticizing – are all socially useful, in the nature of *work*, but that the gain over the narrowing effects of a division of labour results from mobility, so that a person doesn't sink his entire life into one narrow activity but is free to move from one to another and thus achieve an all-sided development of himself by not identifying with any particular occupation. Whichever of these two interpretations we accept, we find Marx placing his hopes for the future in eliminating the tendency of capitalist society to force upon people a particular occupation as a life pursuit. Regardless of whether his dominating image is that of a leisure- or a work-oriented society, the leading idea is that of mobility among occupations so that people don't identify with any particular life pursuit. Consequently, we should not expect Marxists to be attracted to the ideal of a professionalized society.

Ordinarily, professionals do what they do more competently than amateurs. The fisherman who is trying to catch fish because he is of a mind to and will shortly turn to some other activity, is not going to catch as many fish or catch them as expertly as will a person who has resolved to *be* a fisherman. If all we were thinking of were the results of activity – the number of fish caught, deer shot, cattle bred, or writers criticized – it would be easy to reply to the objection that Marx envisages an inefficient society by noting that the quality of

long paragraph in *Capital*, III, where Marx distinguishes between the realm of necessity (the sphere of work) and the realm of freedom. These texts don't challenge the view that Marx, like the Chinese 'leftists,' distrusted 'experts' and preferred amateurs. But they do suggest that Marx's ideal society is fundamentally leisure-oriented and that for Marx the great contribution of capitalism is that it develops the technology without which a fully leisure-oriented society cannot emerge, while its crippling contradiction is that it constantly frustrates this outcome by converting leisure time into surplus labour: 'Thus, despite itself, [capitalism] is instrumental in creating the means of social disposable time, and so in reducing working time for the whole of society to a minimum and thus making everyone's time free for their own development. But although its tendency is always to create disposable time, it also converts it into surplus labour.' *The Grundrisse*, ed. and trans. D. McLellan (New York, 1971), p. 144.

life is more important than efficiency. There are, however, two strong reasons for rejecting Marx's image of a society of amateurs and replacing it with the ideal of professionalism.

1 Among people who do something well there is realization that it is worth doing well. The difference between an amateur and a professional isn't just that the latter gets better or more results but that he gets the results as they should be got. He shows excellence in the activity itself. By so doing he makes an immediate contribution to the quality of life. To think of there being no fishermen and no hunters, only people who now and again fish and hunt, is romantic, but attractive only so long as we think of it abstractly, stressing people's freedom to pass from one activity to another at will but ignoring the quality of the actions they engage in along the way. Once we recognize that living is acting, so that the quality of a life is largely the quality of the actions it falls into, we must see Marx's view in the way we do that of the film-maker who ruins his film by becoming over-anxious that his actors enjoy themselves while making it.

It may be objected that Marx's dominant ideal was not the amateur but renaissance man: the person who hunts, fishes, breeds cattle, and writes literary criticism, all in the same day, may be seen, that is, not as a dabbler or dilettante but as many-talented. Note that if we drop off the last-mentioned talent, the pattern of life suggested by the other three – hunting, fishing, breeding – isn't as exotic as Marx, a city boy, appears to have believed. No doubt numerous farmers around the world budget their daily round so as to engage more or less routinely in all of these pursuits and many more besides. Marx might say that the difference between such farmers and his wide-ranging person in communist society is that the latter decides to hunt, or fish, or breed *spontaneously*, not under the constraint of needing to earn a living. And it should be acknowledged also that in the passage quoted Marx says that 'each *can train himself* in any branch he wishes.' This suggests not so much a dabbler as a jack-of-all-trades – which is what renaissance man becomes if, unlike Leonardo, he doesn't quite bring it off.

But it is especially Marx's adding that the man who hunts, fishes, breeds, and criticizes nevertheless is never to become a hunter, fisherman, herdsman, or critic that suggests the image of communist society as a society of amateurs. If one is genuinely many-talented – as renaissance a man as his circumstances permit – and, say, well and truly learns how to hunt, fish, breed, and criticize, then thereby he becomes, all in one person, hunter, fisherman, herdsman, and critic. It won't do to reply that by denying these descriptions (by denying, that is, that the person who hunts is a hunter) Marx was not intending to deny that the individual in communist society is to have numerous highly developed talents, but only intended to indicate that he is not forced to spend all his time exercising just one of them. For, that the person is to be doing many different things, if he is of a mind to, is already understood. In effect, a distinction is made between one who hunts, fishes, etc., but is *not* a hunter, fisherman, etc.; and one who hunts, fishes, etc., but moreover *is* a hunter, fisherman, etc. And the only apparent sense the distinction has is that between people who dabble at what they do and people who are genuinely many-talented.

Whatever the final resolution of this issue, however, it is important to grasp the relationships among three ways people may relate with their occupations: the amateur, the professional, and renaissance man. The amateur does many things, moving from one to the other as interest wanes and pleasure is promised elsewhere. The values he seeks aren't those we associate with tasks well done, objects finely wrought, skills in performance. Rather, they are the values we associate with 'creativity': it is the opportunity to 'express himself' that motivates him. The professional, if he has but one profession, has one distinctive talent, one occupation, and aspires not so much to 'express himself' as to do excellently what the profession contemplates. This needn't involve simply following an antecedently prescribed practice, since the practice oughtn't to be a recipe and it is also subject to development. Consequently, in a profession creativity takes a different form; it is not a matter of one expressing oneself but of bringing a talent to bear in an innovative way. The difference is that between, in self-expression, referring an action back to its source in the active individual and judging it by what it does for or to him; and referring the action 'forward' to its object, what it issues in, and judging it by an estimate of that.

If our idea of renaissance man is to be adequately differentiated from that of the amateur, then it must essentially involve being many-talented, and living a life in which many things are done, but all *seriously* and, so far as possible, well. This is to say that renaissance man is simply the man who has not one but many professions. The difference is quantitative; there is no difference in the character of his performance or commitment. Thus, except to note the obvious dangers of people spreading themselves too thinly, and thereby ending not with many talents but with none, I have no objections to register against the ideal of renaissance man and sense no tension between it and the model of an objective, professionalized society. The social commitment, after all, is to create significant occupational opportunities, not to sort people into their occupations. If they choose to lead one life, two, or many - that is their choice, their affair, and their consequences.

2 The second objection to Marx's image of a society of amateurs is more far-reaching. It is crucial to Marx's proposal that people not identify with the particular things they do. In saying that the one who fishes is not to *be* a fisher-

man, Marx may have meant that he is not to live and conceive his life so that he identifies him*self* with fishing. A specialized occupation such as fishing or hunting develops and expresses only a narrow range of a person's human potential. Apparently, then, his identifying with one occupation closes off many facets of his make-up and condemns him to a onesided development as a human being and to a onesided life as well. It seems natural to say, with Marx, that since a person *is* not, simply, a fisherman or a hunter, it is a dangerous mistake for him to identify with either occupation, and a serious fault in a society that it forces such identifications on the majority of people.

Where occupations are of the sort Marx must have had uppermost in mind – narrow not merely in the sense of involving a highly specific type of activity but also in the sense of bringing into play a narrow range of a person's capabilities – and, moreover, where they are not freely chosen from a broad field of genuine options but are imposed by the accident of having been born in such-and-such a place of such-and-such parents, then Marx's conclusion is plausible. Far better that one should become instead an amateur who does many different things at his pleasure and identifies with none of them. But the indicated circumstances need not obtain: there are occupations that are not at all narrow in the sense of bringing into play a narrow range of a person's capabilities, and there is no reason why the line of work a person follows could not become an option freely taken up from a broad field of alternatives that he might have opted for instead.

The practice of medicine, for example, is a highly specialized activity, but it nevertheless calls into play most sides of a person's make-up. It does so by bringing most of his capabilities to bear on a narrow range of concerns. When the issue is whether an activity encourages full development of a person's capabilities, what counts is the extent to which those capabilities are activated, not the degree of specialization or narrowness of the activity in a social context. A professionalized society should be one in which though occupations are specialized it takes whole persons to perform them competently. Achieving this result involves the manner in which the occupations are institutionalized, and is compatible with their being highly specialized and with people totally identifying with them.

Let us imagine that a person who practises a highly specialized craft does identify with it. He not merely fishes but totally identifies himself as a fisherman and is wholly absorbed in his occupation. What could be meant by objecting to his conceiving himself in this manner by observing that fishing is after all just something that he does and that he ought not to confuse himself, the real person who happens to fish, with his role as a fisherman? It is often imagined that there is a final distinction between a person and his role in the world, the latter a kind of mask the person stands behind, so that to identify with the role is to practise self-deception and to encourage others as well to mistake one thing for another.

But the image of a person with a mask only fits a special case. Where a person's occupation has no deep roots in his capabilities and aspirations, then in carrying it on he is scarcely expressing him*self*. In these circumstances, to act as though he identified with it would be for him to profess to be a kind of person he is not and it would be natural to refer to the occupation as a 'role' in the sense of a mask behind which the real person hides. But either the person expresses himself in some other activity with which he *does* identify or his capabilities and aspirations have found no adequate outlet. In the former case the objection is not that he identifies with something that he does, on the basis that what he is and what he does (his role) are two different things. It is rather an objection to the particular occupation by reference to which he defines himself. And in the second case the solution is not for him simply to step out from behind the mask and present his true face to the world. He needs rather to find another occupation that does catch up his capabilities and aspirations and with which he can identify.

To apply this to Marx: he notices that people are cast into narrow, specialized roles to which they are bound for life and, rightly, is repelled. But his solution is simplistic. He envisages a society in which no one identifies in a deep way with any specialized pursuit but passes from one activity to another without developing intensive competence for any. In a profession-oriented society, by contrast, the person identifies with a specialized pursuit to which he may very well bind himself for life. But because this is a pursuit that activates his capabilities and through which his aspirations seem capable of fulfilment, his identification with it signifies not self-deception but self-fulfilment.

IV

A person's identification with a professional activity may occur on three levels, on each of which he establishes a relationship the absence of which involves alienation. He identifies with himself, his occupation, and his colleagues. In each case the identification has two sides. It consists in a settled feature of his life, objectively considered, and in his outlook upon his life, by which he consciously realizes that feature. Since the three levels of identification are interrelated in one life situation, it will be best to begin by describing that situation and then isolate the three levels within it. We are to imagine that a person has found a 'life work' that is professionalized and in which he finds a broad spectrum of his capabilities engaged. The activity this calls forth is admirable in kind and competently carried out. In it he experiences the central meanings of his life, and finds dignity through realization that the occupation is valuable and serious and that this is publicly recognized through the support he receives in order that he might carry it on. Professionalization of the occupation involves that he has recognizable colleagues with whom he interacts and whose life situation is comparable to his own. They have comparably developed competences and locate the central meanings of their lives in the same objects.

In this idealized state of affairs, the person's conscious identification with himself consists in his awareness and acceptance of his distinctive competences and aspirations. He recognizes himself in these and experiences them as forming a whole person. This realization on his part is but the reflection in consciousness of the fact that he exists in the world in that way. Where such identification is lacking, as when one represents himself to others as something other than what he is, and in this deception deceives also himself, a person is alienated from himself.

Overtly, a person's identification with his occupation involves that in this activity his distinctive competences and deepest aspirations find a natural expression. He consciously identifies with the occupation by recognizing and accepting that this is so. Not uncommonly, people notice that the central activities of their lives are not even approximate expressions of what they distinctively are. They do not find or identify themselves in their life work because what they are does not in fact show through there. In this alienation from their occupation their lives lack, and are experienced as lacking, focus. A natural result is the continuing sense that one is marking time, waiting.

Finally, that a person's occupation is professionalized means that he has professional colleagues who similarly identify with themselves and their central activity. The result is that they all do in fact exist as a 'community': through their common dedication to the same objectives and pursuits they are brought together in a real unity grounded not in the enthusiasms of individuals but in their life situation. A person's conscious identification with his colleagues is but his realization and acceptance of this unity in the life situation they share. Identification of this sort does not establish a group defined by its distinctness from other groups, so that loyalty to it leads to defending its interests against those of other groups. The group it constitutes rather is defined by its manner of acting *in* the world, and professional identification brings a commitment to assure that that action is characterized by excellence. Consequently, the 'community' formed by identification with professional colleagues is not a closed one and does not depend for its success on the failures of others. Where there is no identification of person with person at all, or where the identifications are based on interest and serve to separate people into opposed groups, alienation is inevitable. Each person either knows no real continuity with any of the rest, or by identifying with some he alienates himself from others. Professional identification may not prompt a vivid sense of continuity with others beyond the immediate circle of professional colleagues. How far beyond that circle toward mankind as a whole the continuity is felt will no doubt depend on the imagination of the person concerned and his capability of imaginatively overreaching his immediate life situation. But the objective orientation implicit in a professionalized life at least points him toward sensed continuity with people generally and beyond that with nature at large. It is for this reason that leisured performance of professional activity may be seen as the appropriate focal value for a society of people who wish to give prominence to the fact of man's continuity with man, with living things, and with nature.

V

The validating experiences of an Objective Society are those in which the foregoing three modes of identification are intensely experienced in leisurely activity. This involves a coupling of leisureliness with awareness of larger meanings, of delight in the present with the sense that it is drenched in significance. Such experience would validate a social system only in case it were and were seen as a natural outcome of the normal functioning of the system, supported and encouraged by the arrangement of affairs.

Consider, for example, a dancer in full possession of his art. He is aware of and takes delight in the fact that he *is* a dancer. He senses that he finds himself and the life appropriate to him in dance, and experiences a bond of fellowship with those of his associates who are similarly committed. In dance, when it is leisurely, not a struggle to develop his art further but an unhurried expression of what he has achieved and is, he locates the experiences that uniquely validate the arrangements that make his life possible.

The heroes that the model of an Objective Society picks out, then, will be such as Pablo Casals, Pablo Picasso, Bertrand Russell, and Fernand Point, people who had a *profession* and lived lives that were true to it. Each reached a stunning development of his talents that he saw as a gift, was led by this perception to a sense of responsibility to express his talents so long as his physical capabilities permitted, and took delight in the leisured activity that ensued.

The ideal of a professionalized society has many points of continuity with existing trends. Specialization and professionalization are natural accompaniments of an advancing technology. What mainly distorts them is the dominant role of interest in our lives, particularly as institutionalized in 'business.' Although one can imagine that something approaching the ideal described could be approximated as a result of a pervasive revolution in consciousness, without, in the first instance anyway, corresponding institutional changes occurring, it is more realistic to concentrate on the overt social transformation on which such a revolution would largely depend. Accordingly, in the following chapter I shall attempt to identify some steps by which an Objective Society might be brought into being.

CHAPTER NINE

From work to professionalism

In most people's lives, as in society at large, a fairly clear demarcation exists between the spheres of work and leisure. But not everyone agrees concerning the sphere that is most important, within which a person may feel he really lives as opposed to merely preparing for life. At one extreme, leisure is seen as all-important and work is accepted as making leisure possible. At the other, people live in their work and regard leisure as, literally, recreation, time for renewing energy so they may return to work. Just as there is no consensus concerning which sphere is most important, so do most of us vacillate. Unable to opt for either extreme, we seek primary meanings now in one sphere, now in the other, the movement from one to the other accelerated by discovery that neither fulfils its promise. We often experience each sphere as the negation of the other – work as the time we are not at leisure, not our own person, leisure as the time we have no need to work. Moving back and forth between the two is like a series of escapes. Lacking positive significance, leisure soon becomes ennui or boredom, propelling us to work, and work in its turn becomes onerous, monotonous, or directed toward ends that threaten self-respect, propelling us back to leisure. Professionalism and leisureliness in the Greek sense may be seen as means of bringing positive significance to the two spheres. Professionalizing work involves giving it a character that makes it possible and sensible to locate the primary meanings of life there. And to occupy free time in a leisurely manner is to vest it with meaning independent of one's occupation, so that it loses its largely negative aspect.

Just as it is not particularly helpful to advise someone to relax, so is the advice 'Be professional!' or 'Be leisurely!' largely empty. But a physician who discovers that his patient ought to relax more may think of changes in the patient's lifestyle that are in his power to make and that might have the desired effect. Similarly, with regard to professionalism and leisureliness there are institutional changes an affluent society has the resources to make which would go a long way toward facilitating the required shift in lifestyles. Whether we are prepared or able to make the changes is a different matter, of course. In this chapter I intend to discuss the sorts of changes suggested by the idea of professionalism, in the following chapter those suggested by the idea of leisureliness.

For the most part we have sufficient technological resources for making the sorts of changes I shall refer to. We have the technical ability and level of productivity that would be required to largely professionalize the economy. The main obstacles seem to be political and psychological – and these are extremely large obstacles indeed. Whatever the correct analysis of power in Western society, it is not at all likely that those who wield it would find the suggestion that we should professionalize the economy one they can act on. And, on the psychological side, the attitude toward work implied by the idea of a professionalized occupation is so at odds with the expectations of the great majority of people who work that nothing very much, all at once, could possibly be accomplished.

The following remarks, therefore, are not policy proposals. Neither do they identify a final goal that we should march toward, a utopia we should try to bring down from the heavens and make real here, now, or tomorrow. In part, rather, they are intended to give content to the idea of professionalization. And for the rest they may serve to light up a path, to pick out of the gloom a direction and give some sense of where it leads without supposing that the end of it can be seen, much less reached. It is important that we should be able to move that way, though.

II

We may think of the 'economy' as a network of occupations. To professionalize it is to make changes that accelerate a shift in the character of occupations from their being forms of work to their being modes of professional life. Such a shift would involve changes in the structure of occupations, considered as social practices, and changes in the people who carry them on. A professionalized occupation is distinguished by autonomy; by the fact that it is not self-referring but is directed toward an objective that is generally desirable or admirable; and by its dependence on a specialized competence, a 'method' for the acquisition of which, typically, people require a prior period of training or study, whether as an apprentice or through formal education. From the other side, people carry on an occupation in a professional manner when they have adequate possession of the relevant competence, function autonomously in expressing it, and are principally motivated by the sense that the ideals associated with the life they are engaged in and its results are themselves admirable and worth pursuing per se.

1 Making an occupation autonomous involves altering the practices by which it is controlled so that the decisions regarding how a person is to carry it on – what he is to do and how, when, and where he is to do it – are made by him. In the great majority of cases, unlike much medical and legal practice, an occupation makes no sense in isolation but is conceived as a specialized role in a cluster of related occupations that co-operate in producing an object, a house, say, or an automobile. Here autonomy refers not merely to the situation of the individual but to that of the working group as well. Although there are serious difficulties associated with reconciling the autonomy of the individual with that of the group he works with, and compromises are probably always necessary, this does not discredit the idea that an attempt at reconciliation should be made. Think of a group of doctors, all of whom are specialists in a different aspect of medical practice and who are co-partners in a clinic. And, in a joint activity that requires a command post and lines of authority – a commando team, for example, or the captain and crew of a boat or airplane – a person's autonomy within the command structure may nevertheless be reasonably assured by the facts that his participation in the group is voluntary and the part he plays is not overly routinized or dominated by the external authority.

But by all odds the principal tactic suggested by the need to reconcile the autonomy of the individual with that of the group his occupation primarily involves him with is decentralization of the group. The smaller the group, and the more complete its distinctive contribution to the complex enterprise it is tied to, the more feasible both to allow it to function autonomously within the larger enterprise and to allow the individuals the group contains to function autonomously within it. The current movement toward reanalysing mass production processes into segments for which work teams are responsible is an important if small step in the right direction. Sometimes the advantages stressed are that in a work team the impersonality of the mass production line and the isolation of workers from one another are eliminated, and that *esprit* within the work team might develop which would lead to greater efficiency. But the most important consideration is that the workers are enabled to function more autonomously so that they may regard their occupation as *theirs* and, if it is otherwise admirable, identify with it and in it affirm themselves and their dignity.

2 The two principal reasons why occupations and the economy as a whole are self-referring are that they are subordinated to the profit motive and that the extrinsic rewards for the sake of which they are carried on largely serve to decorate the private spheres in which people live. Typically, people in an occupation, motivated by extrinsic rewards, are employees, while the employing firm exists in order to make a profit and directs the employees' activities with this

end in view. As a result, their occupation is likely to be distorted from two sides. Often their immediate concern is not to do properly and well what the occupation involves, but merely to get by with minimum effort and attention. And the uses to which the occupation is put by the firm are frequently rather different than they would be were it directed by the sense that it is a profession defined by ideal standards that all concerned aspire to measure up to. Because this is so, it may be quite sensible for them not to take the occupation very seriously. The two ideas, that it would be desirable for people to identify with their occupation so that it becomes a life work to which they devote themselves and in which they gain their sense of the importance of their time on Earth, and that the occupation should not be distorted by being subordinated to a profit motive, go hand in hand.

It is, of course, possible to retain occupational integrity within an economy directed by the profit motive. Although we may doubt that our economy manages this to any significant degree, one can envisage a development of it in which, without departing from its basic capitalist character, occupations become largely professionalized and the people who carry them on do so in a professional manner. This would involve profit becoming a condition rather than a dominating objective. For example, the manager of a small retail business might very well take the view that he is performing a service for the community by having on hand commodities that are well made and of genuine use to his customers. He may be quite careful in his business activities to assure that this remains the case. And he may adjust his prices with an eye to realizing the small margin of profit he requires to live comfortably and stay in business, having no wish to earn more if that would interfere with the quality of his service to the community. In this way, he would acknowledge that he lives in a community where making a profit is a condition of staying in business, but would not subordinate his sense of how best to carry on his business, taking into account community needs and his own convictions about the occupation he is in, to the objective of maximizing profit. And it is not difficult to imagine this occurring throughout an entire economy. In the same way, we can readily imagine people on salary who do not regard their income as a reward for painful services but perceive it primarily as one of the conditions making their occupation possible. Since their real interest in life is their work, they are led to see what they receive for working not so much as a *pay-off* as a cover for expenses. Many people today take this view and we can at least imagine a time when, within an economy such as our own, virtually everyone takes it.[1] And so it may be said that there is no necessary incompatibility between capital-

1 One of the many remarkable features of Studs Terkel's collection of views people take toward their work is the frequency with which they invoke the idea of 'profession' in describing either what they like about their work or what they regard it as primarily lacking. *Working* (New York, 1975).

ism and the profit motive, on the one hand, and professionalism, on the other.

But even if one were convinced of the real possibility of reconciling professionalism and the profit motive, which I am not, one would need to understand the steps by which, within the existing system, the union would have to be realized. And the most natural way to come to this understanding is to suppose instead that professionalism is to be pursued by carrying out rather basic changes in our economic institutions, so that rather than existing within a capitalist economy it appears as a distinct economy that replaces capitalism. Then, in light of this pure form of a professionalized economy, one may if one wishes look back to the project of purifying capitalism with a clearer view of what is required. What would emerge, I think, is realization that practically speaking there is no difference between committing oneself to the professionalization of occupations within a capitalist economy and committing oneself to professionalism as a distinct, post-capitalist economy. The concrete steps one ought to take in pursuit of the first of these commitments are much the same as those one ought to take in pursuit of the second.

III

The possibility of professionalizing an economy is created by advanced technology. So long as human labour must largely be used to capacity in assuring satisfaction of rather basic needs, there is little scope for adapting occupations in the ways suggested by the ideal of professionalism. Increased productivity introduces new options with respect to the organization of occupations, principally because economic efficiency becomes a less serious consideration. We may begin, then, by asking why in general these options aren't being taken up to any appreciable extent.

Two of the main factors are these: first, whether a new technology that would diminish the labour intensivity of a productive activity is perfected and introduced depends on the profitability of such an innovation to the firm concerned; and, second, whether the workers affected will accept or resist it depends on its felt implications for their own life prospects. If the proposed innovation is not narrowly profitable, or if organized labour finds it threatening, then there is little chance of its being accepted. The advantages that might accrue if these bars to labour-saving innovations, in particular automation, could be overcome are incalculable. From the standpoint of the ideal of professionalism, the reason for this is that the occupational changes implied by the ideal depend for their feasibility on extensive automation, used not as a means of increasing efficiency but rather as a way of creating space in the economy within which people's occupations can be professionalized.

Let us suppose, contrary to fact, that currently all occupations are carried on as work, in pursuit of extrinsic rewards, and involve minimal autonomy and identification because they are subordinated to a profit motive. Then let us suppose that the bars to automation and to other labour-saving technological innovations are removed, but that these innovations are introduced not with an eye to improving efficiency or profitability but as a means of creating space in the economy so that professionalism might be enhanced. Suppose, that is, that professionalism is taken seriously as an ideal and that a serious, concerted attempt to convert the economy is made. By some procedure or other, decisions would need to be taken concerning which occupations are to be professionalized. The critical test would be whether anyone chooses to take the occupation up, in circumstances where the reason for doing so is not extrinsic, such as the promise of monetary return, but lies instead in the quality of life the occupation immediately involves. We shouldn't think of these decisions being made all at once, in some Master Plan for the society as a whole, nor should we imagine that they would be made by a centralized authority. Rather, they would be made by the people themselves as they confront the choice of a life work, without being constrained by the requirement that through this work they are to earn their 'living,' if at all. In these circumstances, many current occupations would simply lapse, and many more would certainly be drastically modified. The principal role of automation would be to make it possible for the society to meet its needs despite these profound changes in the uses to which people put their productive energy or 'labour power.' We need some view of (1) the mechanisms by which people would sort themselves into their occupations, and (2) the manner in which society would react to the fact that some occupations are abandoned.

1 Two sets of practices are indicated. First, a guaranteed income floor is required by which every person is assured a reasonable standard of living. This is often defended, but ordinarily on the basis that everyone has a 'right to life.' Here, however, the more serious view is taken that the income floor represents the minimum needed for *any* occupation or life work. If the society is to commit itself to offering everyone an opportunity to find a profession in pursuit of which he affirms himself and his dignity as an active creature, then it must somehow assure everyone that his standard of living will not fall below a reasonable level. To refer to this as an 'income' floor is admittedly an oversimplification, since the object is to assure a minimal but reasonable quality of life, some of the elements of which are public goods not obtained through expenditure of personal income.

The second set of practices indicated are those that determine access to the special resources needed in order to carry on a professional activity in a responsible manner. These are of two sorts – educational practices, by which competence to carry on the activity is gained, and those that provide the means of carrying it on once the competence has been acquired. The latter involve resource allocation, including space, equipment, and material, but also interpersonal relations of the relevant sorts. Although not all occupations should be viewed as producing a service or commodity, few if any are possible or even intelligible when carried on in a social vacuum. Philosophers don't have clients, or patients, or customers, but the 'product' of their activity is an object in a social space created by the perspectives and concerns of the philosophical community. Only in such a space does it come alive and work. Had Henry Moore been a Robinson Crusoe without a man Friday, and peopled his island with two-piece reclining figures and the like, the world would have had in it the same exquisite forms it now enjoys. But the lack of contact between these forms and the community of people responsive to sculpture, necessary in order that the forms might gain their appropriate place in the world, would have meant that they were like crates in a warehouse, a stockpile, the potentiality for something not yet achieved. What one needs in the way of resources for carrying on a life work is a structuring of social space that opens the field in which that work and its results may exist publicly. At its core, depending on the character of the work, this means customers, clients, patients, an audience, or colleagues, in relation with whom the work proceeds. (This is no more to say that the object of art is to communicate than it is to say that properly the object of producing commodities is to make a sale.) And generally the possibilities for excellence in the work are closely tied to the special characteristics of such people, the character of their problems, sensitivity, or intellect, so that all of the additional factors that shape such characteristics are further resources needed if occupations are to prosper.

The problem of resource allocation is subtle, not simply a matter of deciding how to provide and distribute the immediate requisites for carrying on an occupation but also one of conceiving programs that will enliven the social space in which the occupation and its results must exist. These two aspects of the problem are best considered separately. The most straightforward, if stupid, way of determining the distribution of immediate requisites – equipment and material – would be to create a centralized agency as a kind of projects approval board, with functions analogous to those of committees responsible for evaluating research grant proposals. In most cases, people would be engaged in occupations the needs for which are broadly predictable, so that initial decisions concerning individual cases or antecedently established principles would continuously apply and for most people gaining resources to carry on their life work would be analogous to receiving a fairly automatic renewal of a research grant – work in progress. The resources allocated would be an output of the occupation itself (to which extent it would be self-maintaining), or of other occupations, or of the automated portion of the economy, and would be regarded as first entering a common pool of social wealth. Some of this would be needed to provide the income floor; some, to enliven the social space in which occupations exist; some would be devoted to savings against future contingencies; and some would be expended to underwrite and improve the quality of leisureliness in the spheres of individuals' lives to which professionalism doesn't reach. The remainder would be redistributed to sustain professional activity.

Once the system was operating, most decisions regarding occupational support would concern people just entering upon their life work, people who have come to feel that they wish to change their occupation, or people who have developed their occupation in innovative ways, creating new needs for carrying it on. Whether it is easy or hard to accommodate these needs would be determined by the scarcity of the social wealth available for distribution. The Russian economy operates in something like this way, except that the overriding objective in determining levels of occupational support is not that of creating and sustaining a professionalized economy. Rather, to a large extent, the occupations are made to serve national goals and they are, moreover, excessively bureaucratized. Nevertheless, much of what goes on there seems compatible with the goal of professionalism. Whatever the Party's motives may be for its lavish support of athletic programs, for example, the result is that athletes are established as professionals. A field of activity is blocked out for them and they are provided with the conditions needed in order that they might excel in it. Often it seems clear that the athletes are dedicated to perfecting their performance in the sport they have chosen and that their personal orientation stresses values imputed to the activity at hand, not national goals or personal advancement.[2]

2 When applied to athletics the terms 'professional' and 'amateur' are ambiguous in parallel ways. 'Professional' means both carrying on the sport for monetary reasons and taking it seriously in the way suggested by talking about a 'life work.' And 'amateur' similarly means both carrying on the sport with no promise or thought of monetary reward and not taking it entirely seriously by striving somewhat single-mindedly to excel in it. Both meanings of 'amateur' are sometimes put positively by talking about the amateur practising the sport 'for the love of it,' and of course the etymology of 'amateur' suggests this usage. Although it makes some sense to contrast practising a sport for financial reasons – 'professional' in the first sense – with being motivated by love of the sport itself, it makes no sense to oppose practising the sport in a serious way, identifying with it, striving to excel in it – 'professional' in the second sense – with being motivated by love of the activity the sport involves. For in this sense it is the professional more than any other who does love his sport, and so is truly an

By envisaging decisions regarding distribution of resources for carrying on an occupation as being made by a centralized agency, we are able to bring into one uncluttered view the reorientation of human activity implied by the principle of professionalism. A practicable decision mechanism, however, would need to be extremely complex. We needn't attempt to elaborate the details of such a mechanism here, but it should be said that it might depart from the simplified scheme suggested by the foregoing remarks in both of two directions. Decisions concerning resource allocation might be made by impersonal mechanisms, as in competitive markets, or by decentralized, local groups in which everyone in some manner participates. The first of these is, or is compatible with, professionalism within a capitalist economy and would probably require income controls that limit wages and profits more or less to the level suggested by the principle that the use of income is that of underwriting a professional life. The second suggests a community structure comparable to the organization of communes in China, but with each local unit incorporating a variety of occupations and working groups and deciding collectively how their own share of the society's wealth is to be distributed among them. The appropriate mix of these three approaches – centralized decisions, local community decisions, and impersonal decisions through competitive markets – reflects such factors as a society's homogeneity, the sophistication of its technology, its level of affluence, and the strength of the family structure, so that not much can be said about it in a general way beyond noticing that there are dangers associated with each of the three approaches when it is stressed to the exclusion of the other two.

In large measure, the subtle factor of social space cannot become a policy objective but must arise as a happy side-effect of other pursuits. In this area, success breeds success. Most countries have one city where creativity in the arts is most vital and where most of the ferment is to be found. The other large population centres tend to be, by contrast, wastelands. Compare Liverpool with London, Lyons with Paris, Pittsburgh with New York, Hamilton with Toronto. The obvious explanation is that once one centre has sprung up it acts like a centripedal force, drawing to it most of the potentiality for creativity that first appears elsewhere. Attempts to counter such forces, by nurturing

'amateur.' His being paid *in order that* he might practise the sport should not be condemned but encouraged, since the effect is to release him so that he can pursue the activity he is dedicated to without distraction. It is simply evidence of confusion in basic ideals that the Olympics program attempts to discourage subsidizing athletes, in effect supposing that there would be some virtue in bringing together once every four years masses of young people from all over the world to compete in sports that are for them essentially sideline activities. What saves the program is that the principle isn't followed through. But the hypocrisy this involves is scandalous and itself taints the program.

creativity in provincial cities, are likely to yield distorted results – caricatures or excessively derivative products. The reason is that to succeed the activity should be spontaneous, but all too often the artist is not in contact with his own creative impulses but is casting his eye abroad for models to be guided by. In occupations generally the social milieu in which they are carried on should exude the expectation and conviction that one will practise it with integrity and that there is room for and acceptance of the results of doing so. One may hope that policies that minimize the domination of extrinsic motives – subordination of the occupation to national goals, to the pursuit of profit, or to the desire to 'earn a living' – would contribute to this milieu. But for the most part it must be seen as something that people themselves, acting conscientiously in their occupations, bring to life. At first, all we should expect is a number of small, precarious flames. Whether they persist and finally spread to the point where they can assure their own growth will perhaps lie in the lap of the gods. But the chance for a vital professionalized society, in which all occupations are alive with a sense of their power and worth, largely rests with the fate of such flames.

Our own history presents a few dramatic instances of the sort of flowering these remarks suggest. One thinks especially of Athens during the fifty-year period between the Persian and Peloponnesian wars and of Italy between, say, 1450 and 1550. It would be ludicrous to draw a parallel between these periods and similar movements in our own era. And yet it is not irrelevant to notice how extensive the enthusiasm for craft and profession has become during the past decade. Throughout North America and Europe numerous craft-oriented 'businesses' have sprung up. The 'businessmen' are frequently occupied with both making and selling their products: pottery, macramé, glassware and stained glass, prepared foods, tapestry and woven goods, furniture, leather goods, etc. Often, the same room serves simultaneously as workshop and sales floor. Small towns and certain districts of large cities have undergone quiet but dramatic transformation as a result of the spread of shops of this sort. The 'businessmen-craftsmen' obviously aren't out to get rich. Rather, one may suppose, they hope to support themselves decently while doing something they believe in. They are fundamentally *craft*-oriented: they are challenged by their craft, strive to perfect it, and take pride in their achievements.

Not all manifestations of this 'movement' involve traditional crafts. Contemporary technologies also are often practised in a non-'business'-oriented fashion. The electronics industry, for example, especially that segment of it responsible for sound reproducing equipment – loudspeakers, power amplifiers, pre- and pre-pre-amplifiers, turntables, tone arms, cartridges, equalizers, cross-overs, etc. – is divided between a few, mostly Japanese, giant corporations and numerous small, craft-oriented companies that attempt to create state-of-the-art equipment. Designers and fabricators of this equipment could probably find more lucrative employment with the giant concerns. Despite the practice of giving each state-of-the-art contender a distinctive brand name or model number, the designer cannot resist constantly fine-tuning his brain-child, with the result that unless one knows the serial number of the individual item and the history of the design innovations one doesn't know whether one owns today's or yesterday's state-of-the-art. No doubt Kenneth Clark and John Curl would disagree regarding the appropriateness of comparing recent developments in this segment of the electronics industry with the Italian renaissance, but the two movements are at least comparable in the degree of vitality they bring to their creative efforts.

Professionalism has far-reaching implications for education. But, as will be seen in the following chapter, we ought not to subordinate all facets of society to the demands of professional life. The need for an independent sphere for leisureliness, with its own immediate values, arises from the fact that a complete life is not typically elicited by one's occupational involvement, even when this is complex in the way suggested by the idea of renaissance man. To bend educational policy and practices to the single goal of nurturing professionalized occupations would be onesided. The topic of 'education for leisure' will be reserved for the following chapter.

Generally, no doubt, occupational education is little more than job-training. This applies to professional training in the conventional sense – medicine, law, and the like; to training in such subjects as engineering, journalism, and city planning; but also to those more or less diffused occupational programs that form the bulk of humanities curricula. The distortions that result reflect distortions in the occupations themselves, their subordination to the state or industry that controls them. When job-training of this sort occurs on the job, as in an apprentice system, it has little significance for the goal of professionalizing the economy, since training received in this way is bound to reflect the existing state and conception of the occupation. When the training is formalized, as when it is carried out in a professional school or university, much depends on the degree of independence of the educational institution. Assuming that the program isn't wholly subservient to the conditions under which the occupation is actually carried on, the challenge is to make effective in the program the idea that the occupation should exist as a profession. This means that while acquiring the skills the occupation requires the students should also be enabled and encouraged to approach the occupation in a critical way, questioning the uses to which it is put and the goals it actually pursues and developing out of this critique a sense of appropriate uses and goals so that they may come to apprehend the occupation in ideal terms, as a way of life that is admirable and which they aspire to live up to. Then as the student comes to define himself by reference to the occupation for which he is preparing, the result will not be a packaged product but an autonomous specialist prepared to insist that the work he takes up bear some discernible relationship with his own developed sense of what it should be. The point here would not be to invoke any *particular* view regarding what is right and wrong in our society. Rather it would be to (1) nurture a critical spirit inspired by the ideal that the occupation should involve an admirable way of life autonomously pursued, and (2) enable people starting out in the occupation to identify with that ideal in a concrete way so that their own day-by-day activity might reflect the commitment it entails.

There would be little advantage in attempting to elaborate these comments by discussing details of curricula and course content. People involved in program planning could readily enough supply details appropriate to their circumstances once the general objectives were clearly grasped and assented to, and these details will differ widely depending on the type of occupation a program refers to. One might reasonably expect to find certain common features, however. First, and most obviously, the program should include work in the theory of criticism, in which attention is focused on methods of evaluating social practices and on criteria for guiding such evaluations. Second, it should include a critical study of the history of the occupation, with stress on changing interpretations of its role in society. Third, it should include study of the possible future developments within the occupation, with reference not simply to new techniques but also to possible new roles the occupation as a whole might assume, their feasibility and worth. Most important, this critical dimension of the program should not be tacked on as a postscript to a set of requirements that primarily focus on technical skills. Instead the skills learned should be largely those shown to be relevant by the critical study.

2 Occupations not spontaneously taken up as involving a serious and admirable way of life would undergo one or more of three possible developments. Some would simply lapse by reason of discontinued demand for their product or service; some would be automated; and the remainder, those that can be neither professionalized nor automated but are none the less needed, would form the residual 'work' segment of the economy.

As a society begins to professionalize its occupations, one might expect a drastic drop in demand for many goods and services currently clamoured for but for which people committed to a professional way of life would have no use. One reason is that much current consumption is obviously motivated by desperation or boredom. People not deeply involved in a continuing line of activity that they are able to regard as serious and as bringing meaning to their lives must at least find distractions, and production of these distractions occupies a considerable portion of the work force. Since it is scarcely possible for the producers to take a serious view of the work this involves, a positive feedback loop exists: the character of the work creates a market for its product, which in turn brings more people into that kind of work, thus expanding the market still further. Opening up occupational alternatives that can be taken seriously would thus break the loop at the point where the demand is created.

A second reason why we may expect that as an economy becomes professionalized the demand for the products of many occupations will collapse is that it would be reasonable, one may say inevitable, for such a society to invest considerably less energy than ours does in advertising and other forms of promotion that serve to create or inflate demand for many goods and services. In a naive and sane view, it must appear simply preposterous that so many people are occupied in tension-charged jobs inducing the rest of us to want all kinds of goods and services that are boring to produce, that don't deeply satisfy us, and that give rise to massive environmental problems.

Occupations for which there is a need but for one reason or another can't or shouldn't be professionalized are precisely the ones for which labour-saving devices should be refined. This is the domain to which technology and 'technique' ought principally to apply. A reorientation of occupations in engineering and applied science (and, therefore, of educational programs in these areas) toward achieving this result forms the major step in their quest for genuine professional status. The principle that automation should be used to meet needs, the meeting of which would otherwise require sinking human labour power in occupations that cannot be professionalized, cuts two ways. It points not only to areas where automation should be encouraged but to other areas where it should be discouraged.

Currently, for example, the possibilities of machine learning are being explored, and a sophisticated technology that contemplates replacing teachers by computers in many educational contexts is under development. Not surprisingly, this is objected to on a variety of grounds. But the typical charge is that there are distinctive values in carrying on the process of learning so that it involves a close, personal relationship between teacher and student. And sometimes this is supplemented by the observation that a person's mentality or character reflects not merely what he has learned but how he learned it, that machine learning breeds machine-like minds. On the other hand, machine learning often gets better results. And of course in the long run substantial economies may be involved. The appeal to economy, coupled with the current passion for refining and instituting 'technique' wherever possible, are probably more relevant to the actual motives behind development of teaching machines than is expectation of improving the learning process. Opponents of automated learning may feel that objecting on the ground that their jobs are threatened is too self-interested. But it has a broader significance: teaching is one of the occupations that people are able to regard as a serious pursuit with which they can identify. It is thus pre-eminently suitable for professionalization. There is or ought to be dignity in it, and although the context in which it occurs often isn't structured so that the teacher is autonomous, it can be so structured. The money and energy invested in developing a technology that would permit replacing human teachers by machines would thus be better invested in enhancing professionalization of the occupation – which would involve changes in the programs by which teachers are certified and changes in the schools in which they teach.

It is anomalous that a highly sophisticated technology for automating the learning process should be under development while work such as that around docks and shipping terminals, which could quite readily be done by computer-directed machinery, is left largely to human labour. Probably few people are able to regard the loading and unloading of ships as a serious life work, and yet the pressures against eliminating the occupation are immense. The vehemence with which even such a relatively crude innovation as containerization is resisted is understandable in light of the fact that it threatens the dockers' source of income. But it is a tragedy that we have so little control over our fate that featherbedding is the most constructive response we can take to the threat to the dockers' livelihood that containerization poses.

Regardless of how successful a society is in eliminating the demand for frivolous goods and services, and in diminishing the amount of human labour required for performing boring, back-breaking, or distasteful tasks, a need will certainly remain for work that no one would voluntarily take up as an intrinsically interesting life pursuit. A perfect match between the lines of activity people pursue from choice and those the society needs in order to maintain a high quality of life is unlikely. In consequence there will always be a segment of the economy that represents residual work for the performance of which people require extrinsic rewards, and we might as well face the fact that in the part of the future that we personally shall experience this segment will be the largest one. In thinking of the split between it and the professionalized segment of the economy, however, we need not suppose that it will be matched by a comparable sorting out of people – some wholly professional, some wholly 'workers.' Although our libertarian bias may suggest leaving open to anyone who prefers the option of working for a wage and nothing more, our egalitarian bias may further suggest that whatever 'work' still remains should be shared by all, distributed through the community on some fair basis. Otherwise our professionalized economy would be élitist in the extreme.

Our own economy has the same three segments: it is in fact professionalized to some degree, some of the work is carried out by non-human 'labour,' and the remainder forms residual work. In this perspective the dominant *economic* objective ought to be, not raising the gross national product, not increasing the number of jobs, not raising the level of wages, but shrinking the residual work segment of the economy while expanding the professionalized segment. It is a very serious question whether a society that organizes and directs economic power as ours does is actually capable of pursuing such a policy.

CHAPTER TEN

The structure of leisure

Among the more prosaic city planners 'neighbourhood' is merely a convenient unit to which to refer physical plans. Confronted by a need to focus their thought on something more compact than 'the city,' they find that thinking of the whole as segmented into a number of neighbourhoods, each about the size and population to require just one elementary school, gives a manageable reference point. When 'neighbourhood' is conceived as an ideal, however, two sharply contrasting manners of developing the city planners' unit are favoured. Some see the neighbourhood as a latter-day equivalent of traditional village communities, while others see it as an amenity that facilitates pleasant use of free time in a consumer-oriented society. The former advocate a design that brings into the neighbourhood opportunities and facilities on which the inhabitants might found a reasonably complete life. The latter seek a refuge, sheltered from the offices and factories where the working day is spent, to which one can retire and be one's own person after the daily grind is over. The first ideal of neighbourhood expresses a preference for collapsing the whole of life into one integral sphere. The second ideal envisages two compartmentalized spheres, one for work and one for free time, but opposes them so that each is a foil for the other: neither makes deep sense in its own terms.

The design suggested by the integral view is generally incompatible with the project of professionalizing the economy. There is no conflict between identifying with one's profession and sensing strong neighbourhood ties, even where the occupational activity and concerns carry one far beyond the neighbourhood's borders. But so far as a person's occupation transcends his neighbourhood, he obviously does not found his whole life there, and when the affairs of greatest significance occur in the professional sphere he must to that extent see the neighbourhood as a domain of largely peripheral practices.

On the other hand, there is real need for a second sphere to complement that in which professional life is carried on. For even in the best of circumstances a profession is a specialized pursuit, not a whole life. Since many facets of a person's character are unlikely to find release in his occupation or occupations, he requires another domain in which they may appear. But the two spheres into which modern life falls – work and free time – are distinguished by contrasts that make no sense once work, having been professionalized, acquires intrinsic significance. Free time means time when benefits earned through work may be finally enjoyed, which assumes that work itself is largely an instrumental activity. And it means time the use of which a person determines simply by consulting his own inclinations, in contrast to his situation at work of bowing to constraints imposed by the character of his 'job.' The autonomy of a professionalized occupation undercuts both contrasts: the professional is 'his own person' in pursuing his life work, and the work doesn't merely serve extrinsic ends but is felt to have its point in itself.

The complement to the 'work' sphere in a professionalized society would be not simply a sphere for enjoyment of free time but one that facilitates true leisureliness in activities in which the non-professional sides of a person's make-up are released. Neighbourhood is a natural locale for such a sphere. The grasp of discipline and method that marks a person in his *professional* capacity forms a fitting, supportive contrast with the ease he experiences in the leisurely life of the neighbourhood.

1 If we think of neighbourhood as the sphere for leisure – in the sense not of free time but of absorption in the present – we shall regard flexibility and openness as its primary design principles. In this way a contrast with the discipline of professional life is established. For impulse to have greater play, the setting of life should encourage spontaneity rather than impose specific courses of action, stances, or moods. Ideally, what people are found doing in their neighbourhood would tell us and them something about the way they currently wish to be in the world, but this is possible only if the neighbourhood, in terms of physical design and social patterns, is marked by far-reaching permissiveness. True leisureliness rests on such a feature, and is achieved so far as a person responds to the openness by making contact with himself, in action, stance, and mood. Then, being at home in the immediacy of the present moment, he casts off busyness and distraction and knows leisure.

Openness applies to social patterns as well as to physical design, whether of buildings or town plan. And it has an aesthetic as well as a narrowly functional aspect. The buildings and physical plan of an open neighbourhood answer to a wide range of tastes and pursuits. The parks and play spaces aren't specifically adapted to particular activities but serve rather as generalized tools that the inhabitants find useful for an indefinite number of purposes. One may think of the difference between giving a child numerous highly structured toys, so that although he has wide choice among many diverse play activities each alternative confines him to a particular manner of occupying himself, and giving him a few kitchen utensils – spoons, pots, and pans – over which his imagination may play, finding an endless number of uses for them, each taken up quite spontaneously and continued just so long as the whim persists.

One of the bad effects of our having dedicated the bulk of the public space in neighbourhoods to use by cars is the sacrifice of openness involved. A street that has much traffic on it is scarcely available for any other purpose, not even that of crossing to the other side. Functionally this leads to considerable confinement. Pedestrians are restricted to the sidewalks, which in turn become structured, single-use facilities. And there are parallel aesthetic implications. The fact of closure and confinement in activity is matched by the feeling, when merely apprehending the scene, that everything is settled and fixed, and a mood of either vague oppression or conformity may settle in. There seem to be signs on all sides, advising what may and may not be done, what the various structures and facilities are specifically *for*. Regardless of whether we respond with a desire to conform to the design or with gloom, feeling the weight of it bearing down and closing in, spontaneity and therefore leisure are lost.

When a street is closed to traffic, to create a mall or a play space for neighbourhood children, the lightness felt by practically everyone who ventures on to the liberated space for the first time cannot be understood simply as a response to provision of a new 'facility.' More than merely an exchange of land uses, there is an opening of the scene. The mall seems not to be merely a new 'pedestrian way.' We experience it as land that welcomes diverse uses, and our step may reflect the sense that something of ourself has been called forth. Typically, the urban environment more nearly resembles the infant's toy box full of games and gadgets designed for specific uses. A wide range of choices is offered, but each pre-packages a particular manner of occupying ourselves and tends to cast us in a passive, spectator role.

Inflexible neighbourhoods form a natural adjunct to the contemporary establishment of leisure as free time. When the chores are finished, whether at the office, factory, school, or home, one confronts a stretch of time that must be filled somehow. In a business- and consumption-oriented society the challenge of leisure to those with capital to invest is to market a product with which people will want to fill that time. Finding something new to offer for this purpose requires conceiving a new manner of filling it, and then designing and promoting a commodity that people will need in order to fill it in that way. Like the child's toy, by structuring an activity the commodity pre-packages free time. As more investors of capital seek a share of the leisure business, increasingly specific packages of activity are introduced. For if the amount of free time is constant increasing the number of alternatives for its use is only possible by specifying with finer and finer detail how that time is to be spent.

From buying canvas and oil paints to try our hand at painting we progress to painting by the numbers; from buying a tent and Coleman stove for a week in the woods we progress to a Winnebago; from a cane pole and can of worms we progress to a 'bass boat' complete with two separate outboards and fish scanner. None of these refinements brings the person more into the centre of his free time activity. His involvement is squeezed out to the beginning, when he chooses one or the other of the packages, and to the end, when payments fall due. The choices concern alternative, sometimes highly ingenious, ways of turning off – our minds, sensitivity, and creative impulses. There is no leisure in this because there is little personal involvement. We are not brought out of ourselves into the present moment because by packaging the time the commodity pre-empts spontaneity. The flow of the leisure activity is guided not by issuing impulse but by the rules of the game, the distribution of the numbers, the layout of the camper, the bleeps on the fish scanner.

An open environment, one that does not structure our time, is most readily achievable in the familiar context of neighbourhood. The much-maligned New Towns, Garden Cities, and Greenbelt towns succeed from this point of view far more than do existing urban neighbourhoods. Culs-de-sac to quarantine the cars, separate foot and bike paths, and small public open spaces for groups of houses to front on and to serve as a common for adjacent residents – these arrangements contribute to an open pattern of land use. The physical space of the neighbourhood is adaptable and welcomes a wide range of uses. The impression that neighbourhoods laid out according to such principles are trying to recapture a lifestyle initially associated with small villages arises from the fact that the physical space of small villages similarly welcomes diverse uses. The openness and, through this, conduciveness to leisure that small places possess is not peculiarly tied to their size, however. The decisive factors responsible for the relative inflexibility of urban settings are centralization and the ubiquitousness of commodities and commercialism. Centralized control *means* inflexibility at the local level and, as we have seen, a commodity-strewn existence is one ordered by those who dream up the commodities. But there is nothing about the urban setting that requires either centralization or commercialism.

The most frequently voiced criticism of Garden City and Greenbelt town design principles is that they lead to sterile *residential* neighbourhoods. This is fair. But the open pattern of land use that results from reorienting residences away from the streets and toward public spaces, and from segregating pedestrian and bike paths from streets, is compatible with a more generous conception of neighbourhood than that held by Greenbelt and Garden City planners. The neighbourhood will be more lively if it contains pubs and restaurants and shops, particularly if these are designed and located so that getting to them and making use of them is a casual affair, easy and without hassle. Their impact on the scene should reinforce the sense that the flow of neighbourhood life is not fixed by the overall physical and social structure but that it is what it is because the people themselves want it that way. Only then is there *life* in the neighbourhood, and without this there is no leisure.

2 Decentralization means shifting *control* of an activity, organization, or institution to the local level, within the neighbourhood. It doesn't necessarily involve control *by* the neighbourhood, functioning as a politically effective unit, but only requires that there be awareness of and sensitivity to its needs, problems, and impulses. What is at issue here is the compatibility of the ideal of a professionalized economy with that of neighbourhood as the domain of leisureliness. Control *by* the neighbourhood, if pervasive, would defeat professionalism. The latter contemplates that the persons who carry on an occupation will be autonomous, while neighbourhood control would in effect establish them as employees of the neighbourhood. By contrast, decentralization that stops short of transferring extensive political power to the neighbourhood is not only compatible with but a necessary condition for professionalizing the economy. Occupational autonomy involves bringing serious decision-making down to the level of the person carrying on the occupation. In this sense, it means decentralization. If the inhabitants of the neighbourhood, functioning as a commune, were to involve themselves in an intimate way in the full range of neighbourhood affairs, as is suggested by extreme forms of the ideal of participatory democracy, then this would both cut into occupational autonomy and introduce centralizing tendencies.

From the standpoint of the ideal of professionalism, 'participatory democracy' needs to be reinterpreted so that it is seen as making two distinct demands. First, when the character of an occupation is such that the objective is reached through the co-operation of a number of individuals who relate with one another as a work team, it is the demand that all involved have a role in guiding the collective activity, limited by the horizons fixed by their occupation. The 'participants' are those responsible for carrying out the activity. Thus users, consumers, and others burdened by the activity's indirect effects are excluded. Often it is not clear where the line between participants and users should be drawn. The dentist's patient is clearly a user, but what of the student? Should he be thought of as a full-blooded 'participant' along with his teachers in an educational community? In this case teachers and students should be thought of as 'colleagues,' a point of view that would lead to deep changes in the schools. Or should he be thought of as a beneficiary of a service provided by the teachers? In this case his claim to influence the activity from which he benefits has a different basis and his 'political' role in the school should be less intimate, more formal. Probably the answer is that 'education' as such doesn't imply either role for students – that of a colleague or that of a user – but that as maturity develops the role evolves. At the beginning the student is best seen as a user or beneficiary (he goes *to* school, where something is laid on for him for a definite period of time, after which he leaves), but gradually his relation with the activity becomes more intimate and the sharp distinction involved in the producer-consumer relationship is softened until he becomes in the complete sense a colleague. The objection to many free schools for young children, and one explanation of their limited success apart from the obvious financial one, is that they impose at the beginning a collegiate relationship between teacher and student that should instead emerge gradually and as a result of the educational process having succeeded. ('Teacher, again today do we have to do what we want to do?') At the other end, the objection to many graduate programs is that persons who are or who ought to have become virtually colleagues are still dealt with as students.

The second demand made by the idea of participatory democracy, then, concerns the status of the user, the consumer, or of the person who merely suffers under the indirect effects of an activity to which he makes no contribution as a participant. Control by such people over the activities they use or are affected by is a means to an end, that of guaranteeing that what we may call 'the user's point of view' is understood and taken into account by those directly responsible for the activity. The object is to reflect the society's interest in an occupation, to assure that there is a reasonable fit between its needs and the manner in which professional autonomy is exercised.

Closely regarded, it is perhaps misleading to identify this second demand as stemming from the idea of *participatory* democracy, since the users, whose interests need to be taken into account, are by definition not themselves participants in the activities they need to influence. The main point to grasp, however, is the different bases for the two demands.

The second demand is especially important at a time, such as ours, when social organizations are being increasingly bureaucratized; that is, when joint activities are analysed into increasingly sharply etched roles formed into tight interactive networks, each role performed by a distinct person who is enjoined both to do precisely what the role calls for and not to usurp the role of anyone else. Merely to organize some joint activities that way requires forgetting about many of the needs of users. And once an activity is so organized, it lacks ability to adapt to idiosyncratic needs or to special or new user interests.

But the second demand is no less important in a professionalized society. Because professionalism basically means occupational autonomy, and the professional is or aspires to be the one who *knows*, there is a very real danger, often unfortunately realized, of insensitivity to users' needs or interests and of intolerance of their fears, foibles, and quirks. The distinction between the two demands makes clear that this danger must be met through establishment of users' interest groups, consumer groups, neighbourhood action groups, in general, of political action groups. Whether these operate independently or within formalized governmental structures, their role is fundamentally political. For this reason the terminological problem referred to might best be resolved by referring to the first demand as that of *participatory*, the second that of *political*, democracy.

Ordinarily, the theme of decentralization is developed in the context of an overriding assumption that the neighbourhood is to form a *unit*. Decentralization of large urban complexes served by centralized services and facilities is thought to involve breaking these up into numerous small neighbourhood units which are more or less self-contained and have definite boundaries. The size of the contemplated units is determined by the answers to such questions as the following: how large a population is needed to support one elementary school? to justify one fire station or police station? to support one shopping centre? to warrant a governing council? And, from the other side, how many people are too many for there to be a reasonable amount of face-to-face contact among all the neighbourhood's inhabitants and a sense on the part of each that he is identified with a tangible and concrete whole?

Pursuit of neighbourhood as a unit rests on the idea that it is to form a spatial community, the confined turf or asphalt on which neighbourliness might occur. Whether the underlying motive is to resurrect in a twentieth-century setting a technological version of village community, with its largely enclosed, integral way of life, or merely a refuge from work and business, the neighbourhood will mark off a collection of people who form the community in virtue of their all having settled there. When people's primary ties are with colleagues in professionalized occupations, however, the basis for conceiving neighbourhood as a unit disappears, except as a matter of convenience for planning purposes. Moreover, no special reason remains for discrete settlements at all, on whatever scale, if 'settlement' is used in the deep sense to refer to a place where a definite number of inhabitants have settled for the purpose of carrying out in their relations with one another a more or less complete round of life.

The fact that a rich life requires, besides a professionalized occupation as the occasion for a life work, a sphere for leisureliness in which the facets of a person's make-up not engaged by his occupation may find expression, does not mean that that sphere must exist for him in a particular place. Neighbourhood, rather, is best understood as a trait or quality of the settings in which leisureliness is achieved. Originally the term *did* refer to a quality of life, neighbourliness, while the usage that refers to a *district* didn't appear until the end of the seventeenth century, some 250 years after the word was introduced into the written language.

To build 'neighbourhood' is to transform the settings in which we live in ways that discourage busyness and distraction and that prompt people to come alive to and become active in their immediate surroundings. Without this, no real interpersonal relationships, neighbourliness, are possible. Above all, successful neighbourhood requires that the surroundings be open, aesthetically and functionally; and openness is enhanced by removing the constraint that the neighbourhood be enclosed within confined borders, since closing off people's rounds of life in this way must involve restricting their access to opportunities they are likely to find attractive.

II

Leisureliness, unlike free time, is something a person achieves, not something he receives. And to this two things are contributory: first, the setting in which it occurs should be congenial; second, the person must be *capable* of leisure. The first was considered under the heading of neighbourhood, regarded as the quality of the human environment that makes it conducive to leisure; the second refers to the role of education.

'Education for leisure' as we know it is training by which a person develops minimal skills for doing things by which he fills, and thus overcomes the boredom of, his free time. He learns wood-working, potting, acting, or book binding well enough so that he can at least do these things in recognizable ways. Then when he is afflicted with free time he has a capability of occupying himself. Since people who lack such capability are in a decidedly unhappy condition, education for leisure in this sense is clearly beneficial. But when we broaden the idea of leisure so that it refers not to free time but to a manner of relating with the flow of time we are bound to broaden our understanding of education for leisure as well. In this broadened sense leisure is an aesthetic stance and mode of relationship with our surroundings, so that education for leisure becomes essentially aesthetic education.

What is meant by an 'aesthetic stance' can best be seen by contrasting it with different approaches to objects. If I watch an athletic contest as a *partisan* the significance of the action for me is coloured by the clues it provides regarding the outcome of the contest. The flow of the game is primarily grasped in terms of a desired or abhorred future event. In the main I only see, only appreciate and react to, features of the contest that contribute to the result, victory or defeat. The same contest, seen by the team's business manager, may present a very different aspect. Now the very ambiguity of the outcome may be a source of comfort, since it creates excitement that will help ticket sales for future games, while winning by a wide margin may be as distressing as losing. An aesthetic stance toward the contest differs from both a partisan and a commercial stance in that now the spectator attends to the game not in terms of its bearing on future events, so that he selects for attention only what is relevant to those events, but instead apprehends it in its own immediate terms. His perception is still selective, but so far as his stance is aesthetic what he selects is not grasped as important in virtue of something outside the game and the setting in which it occurs. He may be particularly responsive to the kaleidoscope of colour presented, the grace of the players, the geometry of the movement, the sheer skill of the teams or of individual players, the rhythms that show through crowd noises and cheers – or all of this at once. But his interest doesn't point him beyond the present event in the plain way that that of a partisan or business-minded spectator does. It wraps him *in* the event.

Aesthetic education in its most general terms is education that nurtures our capability of adopting an aesthetic stance in this sense. It develops a capability of giving ourselves to objects and of discriminating, understanding, and responding sensitively to the objects so that our relationship with them becomes rich, varied, and deep. Since the object may be conceptual rather than perceptual, the thinker absorbed in his thoughts for their sake rather than for their use in solving problems he faces takes an aesthetic stance as well. 'School' derives from the Greek word for leisure, σχολή, and our 'scholar' is, in Greek, 'one who enjoys leisure.' The Aristotelian view that contemplation is the highest form of leisure probably rings true to many contemporary scholars, particularly if they are allowed to broaden Aristotle's notion of contemplation into that of a life of unhurried scholarship.

In the past the traditional subject-matters and disciplines of the liberal arts and sciences supplied the content for 'education for leisure.' Over the centuries the details changed, but the basic orientation and rationale throughout were substantially those first made explicit by Aristotle: the activity most suitable to a free and leisured man is *knowing*, so that education must above all be directed toward development of intellectual virtue. Recently, liberal education has come under serious attack as being 'irrelevant.' 'Relevance' is an ambiguous term in that it refers both to what otherwise is called 'social relevance' and to that which is intrinsically interesting and exciting. In the latter sense to complain that a subject-matter is irrelevant is simply to say that it is not found interesting. Unfortunately, stressing the first of these senses of 'relevance' has prompted an attempt to fasten on to liberal education the task of social criticism, which makes more sense in professional education – unfortunately, since by default it has left occupational education at the sterile level of job-training. So far as the second sense of relevance has prevailed, by leading to introduction of subject-matters of greater contemporary interest, too often the principle has been followed that to be interesting it is necessary to be easy, to make no real demands on students.

In the preceding chapter I sketched some features of professional education and stressed the idea that it should be essentially critical, directed toward developing capability of evaluating the occupation and of reshaping it so that it might become a profession in the ideal sense. In the present chapter I have claimed that education for leisure has no peculiarly critical role in *that* sense but should aim at nurturing the aesthetic mode of relationship with objects. In aesthetic education, criticism means enquiries that open up an accurate, discriminating response to objects taken in their own terms rather than as means to ends.

The upshot of the discussion in this and the preceding chapter is that education has two distinct roles, and it is natural to suppose, in view of the different competences required for carrying them out, that two different kinds of program are required. The current analogues for these at the university level are occupational programs, euphemistically called professional schools, and programs in the liberal arts and sciences. But the fact that two different kinds of program are required doesn't imply that student bodies should also be divided between the two so that by and large they are involved in just one of the two roles. Instead, the line of thought started here suggests the view that a complete education includes extensive involvement in both kinds of program. At present, this is piously assented to but seldom taken very seriously in practice. The usual way in which, for example, engineering programs incorporate a 'humanities requirement' is just comical. But the claim that students should have serious access both to professional education and to liberal education presupposes that the professional education will be something more than mere job-training – which it all too often is – and that liberal education will not be a musty and pedantic regurgitation of empty 'truths' – which it all too often is. Those involved in vocational education are sensitive to the second failing but not the first, while those involved in liberal education are more sensitive to the first than to the second. And both respond by arguing that the educational role of the other group is therefore of lesser importance. But the real implication is that both should look to their own shortcomings – that job-training should become critical and evolve a sense of the professional character of the occupation that forms its subject-matter, and that liberal education should become alive to the peculiar immediacies of the present day, which would involve broadening its scope and vivifying traditional subject-matters.

III

In the foregoing pages I have sketched the broad outlines of a model of the future. The three themes that form it are responsibility, leisureliness, and professionalism. I have tried to indicate why one might prefer such a model to the two our intellectual history naturally suggests to us. And I have sought to define the underlying personal orientation that complements the ideal of a society in which these themes are taken seriously. Finally, I have pointed to some of the major kinds of social change required for there to be any significant realization of the ideal.

One may complain, rightly, that the model is bare and incomplete, many questions left unanswered, many details not filled in. My object has been to say enough to clarify the soul of the ideal. The complete elaboration must be sensitive to the distinctive resources and liabilities of the places where it is to be seriously taken up and must reflect the distinctive aspirations of the people who inhabit those places.

Meanwhile, we see the society around us, the model suggests a state of affairs very different from the one we see, and between a chasm gapes. For the model to make sense, we need to know what might be done with it *now*. In more personal terms, genuine commitment to the ideals the model incorporates assumes some understanding of how that commitment might be expressed. There is a plausible theory of belief that associates belief with action so that if a person never acts on what he purports to believe then it is simply not the case that he believes it. He is just practising self-deception. From this point of view, even *belief* in the model of an Objective Society presupposes knowing some of the ways anyone who believes it might reflect that fact in his own life.

Commitment to a conceived ideal state of affairs can be shown in any of four different ways. These may be classified in terms of two distinctions: that between working from within and from outside the 'system'; and that between attempting to create a better state of affairs as a *result* of one's activity and acting with the intent that the action itself, as opposed to its results, will exemplify the ideal one conceives. The latter distinction involves the difference between being causally effective or 'practical' and being 'idealistic' or acting on 'principle.' These two distinctions give rise to the four ways of showing commitment to an ideal: outside-causal, typified by revolutionaries; outside-immediate, typified by drop-outs; inside-causal, typified by Naderism; and inside-immediate, typified by those in our own society whom I have identified as appropriate heroes for an Objective Society – Casals, Picasso, Point, Russell – most especially the first three, since Russell, more than the others, was an 'activist.'

1 The distinction between operating 'outside' and 'inside' the system is convenient, certainly, but no final theoretical significance should be attached to it. In reality, we have varying degrees to which people interested in changing certain basic practices of a society nevertheless endorse the rest of the established system, and in particular the established procedures for carrying through changes in its practices. Thus, in a democracy the principal significance of oper-

ating 'outside the system' is pursuing change in a non-democratic manner. But in a general way the method involved is that of the revolutionary.

Because of their essentially pragmatic orientation, there is no guarantee that those who seek change in this way will exemplify in their own lives the changes they seek. As a result, their approach contrasts sharply with that of those who show their commitment to an ideal state of affairs by living in a way that immediately exemplifies their ideal. Fundamental character differences are involved here – between those whose primary demand of themselves is that the ideals they hold show immediately in the way they live, and those who demand rather that what they do today shall contribute to a better tomorrow. The position from which the outsider tries to change the system directs him toward attempting to change the power structure, and he is likely to regard further changes as fairly natural and non-problematic consequences of this. Thus, those who seek change in this way may be vague about their goals, considerably more clear about what they oppose.

2 The role of a 'counter-culture' or 'alternative society' is ambiguous. In any case it must be associated with pursuit of change from a position 'outside' the system. But sometimes the motive is to be causally effective, while sometimes it is to live in a way that makes sense in itself without special reference to its social impact. The first approach involves conceiving the counter-culture as a beachhead. A different way of life is established outside the system, or in its interstices, in the hope that the contrast between its evident sense and the emptiness of 'square' lifestyles will start a broad movement that leads to people simply giving up on the established order. Then all the action will be on the side of the counter-culture. Consciousness III seems to have been understood by some in this way; also, Flower Power. But more often the counterculture is understood rather differently, as the attempt to make life meaningful in its own terms, without reference to its social impact. Now one tries to establish within the immediate sphere of his own life a token of the ideal state of affairs he envisages. An example is the person of 'principle' who adheres to his principles despite the likelihood that the consequences of doing so will be generally unpleasant. Regardless of whether the larger motive of using the counter-culture as a beachhead operates, there is no separation of means and ends: the alternative society that forms the immediate concern is so far as possible the end sought, not a mere means to it.

3 People who exist wholly 'within the system' fall into two comparable groups: those who try to be effective in a causal sense and those who simply strive to make their lives a token of the ideal. Some accept the basic rules for bringing about change but perhaps bend them a bit so that they work to their advan-

tage. Tactics play a large role. To be effective it is necessary to calculate, and usually the calculation shows the desirability of adopting rather confined objectives. Such people may be committed to ideals as far-reaching as those that motivate revolutionaries. But their strategy differs. There is no general resolution of the problem 'Is it better to invest energy in a number of small changes that have some likelihood of being accepted or in a quite large change that is improbable?' Personal style and social position largely determine the strategy chosen, and it is likely that a society is better off for having persons of both styles around, the one to push through ameliorations that are feasible, the other to improve the climate of opinion that determines what is feasible.

4 Many people simply live conscientiously. They aren't out to make the world better in any dramatic respect, and they haven't withdrawn their commitment to prevailing institutions. But they have thought about the failings of those institutions, and have attempted within their own sphere to do better. In a job context, where others seem to be just putting in time, they invoke a sense of how the job ought to be performed: they 'professionalize' it. Often this is referred to ambiguously as a person taking pride in his work. Here we aren't interested in the person who merely does conscientiously what is asked of him, but in the one who assumes personal responsibility for the quality of his work. A conception of what is appropriate for the task at hand dominates. What is asked of him may not pass the test, in which case he must balk. His idea is not to reform the occupation, much less the world, but simply to conduct himself, in his own sphere of influence, so that he can hold his head up.

Any of these four ways of pursuing change may be carried through in an objectionable manner or ineffectively, and they may be inspired by ideals we reject. People who seek change from within the system often accept too much, while those who stand on the outside may substitute bitching for action or act in such a gross way that they repel us. People who strive merely to live within their own sphere conscientiously, whether while relating with the established order or outside it, may in fact be shirking a responsibility to have a larger impact on their society. Since profound character differences are associated with the four approaches, there is a tendency to fix on the respects in which people who take an approach other than our own fail. Those who see themselves as standing outside the system sense total opposition to those who seek change from within, and those who regard themselves as *of* the system feel distinctly uneasy in the presence of those who do not. The ways in which particular people fail in pursuing change in their chosen manner are important and need to be kept in view. But awareness of these failings should not blind us to the fact that there is more than one route to the promised land.

It might be more realistic to see the four ways of showing commitment and the lifestyles they involve as simultaneously taken up by the same person. Few are utterly specialized – totally revolutionary and uncommitted to any prevailing practices, or totally committed and in no sense a drop-out. The differences between people on this level are mainly differences in the mix, and in how they choose to present themselves to the rest of us. Nor need this suggest ambivalence or an unsettled mind. If there is something to be said for all of the ingredients of the mix, and it is in the power of a person to be somewhat effective in making contact with his world in all of the mentioned ways, then perhaps he ought to do so.

This seems particularly true in large cities, where numerous specialized environments offer opportunity for a person to combine in one life the roles of dedicated professional, drop-out, community activist, and revolutionary.

1 He may work very hard at his job, have a firm sense of method, and be guided by a vision of truly fine results. And he may have chosen the job in the first place because he saw the possibility of approaching it that way, because it promised a measure of autonomy and he sensed that a life that got its main weight from commitment to it would not be wasted. If (as is likely) his station is a place in a bureaucracy, he pushes at its limits: assumes a responsibility not directly asked; looks beyond the immediate task at hand to the larger system in which he is enmeshed, and rattles it. He may, for example, be Studs Terkel: 'A further personal note. I find some delight in my job as a radio broadcaster. I'm able to set my own pace, my own standards, and determine for myself the substance of each program. Some days are more sunny than others, some hours less astonishing than I'd hoped for; my occasional slovenliness infuriates me ... but it is, for better or worse, in my hands. I'd like to believe I'm the old-time cobbler, making the whole shoe. Though my weekends go by soon enough, I look toward Monday without a sigh.'[1]

2 He may, in addition, inhabit a largely unstructured and unconstrained sphere in which he effectively drops out from the surrounding society and, presumably with others and according to his tastes, enjoys leisure. In this case he holds his dependence on commodities to a minimum, keeping in mind the danger of becoming the urban equivalent of Thoreau's farmer, trudging through life with forty acres on his back. He reads, enjoys music and theatre, perhaps, but especially enjoys the countryside and the opportunity to get thoroughly into it. He knows that the leisureliness of these activities is greatly influenced by the extent to which he is informed; therefore, he has made an effort to become knowledgeable and discriminating regarding the literature, music, and theatre that interest him, and the ecology of the countryside accessible to him.

1 *Working* (New York, 1975), p. xxi.

If his 'job opportunities' have not permitted him to satisfy his urge for *craft* and profession in a way that also earns a living, then in his leisure he may find his craftlife and the job may be just that, a job – in which case we must hope that the hours are short and the work not demanding.

3 He may also be politically active, perhaps within party organizations, perhaps via neighbourhood action groups, concerned especially to assure that his local environment, the urban facilities that are ready to hand and on which the quality of his daily life rests, are sensitive to his needs and those of his friends and form the setting for a tolerable life. He insists on a right to influence his environment, both that in which he works and that in which he seeks leisure. He knows that centralization and bureaucracy in general work against most of the good things he envisages and so is biased toward the small-scale, toward autonomy (for others as well as himself), and toward decentralization of decision-making structures. He is aware of the magnitude of the forces, largely economic, that oppose these biases of his, and is not taken in by the evident good intentions of spokesmen for those forces.

He distrusts blanket solutions, simplistic formulae, encrusted minds. Therefore, although he is deeply *critical* he fears succumbing to knee-jerk liberalism or, if he is a bit younger, to knee-jerk radicalism. Each issue is then, for him, an issue, and he hopes to be saved from the impotence of vacillation by pragmatic commonsense and a warm vision.

4 And he may see as well the imperviousness of his society to radical change by going through approved channels and so play also – however timidly – the role of revolutionary, whether in the individualistic 'up the organization' sense or in the organized manner of revolutionary movements everywhere. Typically, the latter, if serious, is an engulfing commitment that eliminates or considerably diminishes the other three. It makes sense so far as the other three are largely unworkable, otherwise not.

It has been said that ends aren't important, but moving toward them, and having the personal and social power to move toward them, are. This suggests that for the city dweller much depends on whether he can build a life shaped by some mix of the four commitments just described and then in those terms *effectively live.* It isn't much to ask; but it would be plenty to have.

Afterword

Because my intention has been to situate the discussion at the border between theory and practice, in the interest of contributing to the effort to build bridges between the two, I have often pulled back from exploring issues relevant to the underlying normative theory on which the conception of an 'Objective Society' rests. In this Afterword I want to open up some of those issues. The idea is not to 'prove my premises' but to state them, to contrast them with some that are more commonly held, and to suggest some lines of reasoning by which they might be seen as plausible.

For the most part, current value theory has two decisive features: it is input-oriented and man-centred. I shall refer to the first as the dominance of interest, to the second as the dominance of man. By input-oriented is meant that by and large in contemporary value theory values are thought of as a *return*, as something brought to or enjoyed by the creatures who are capable of realizing value. The relevant return is variously described as pleasure; satisfaction of interest, need, or preference; self-realization; fulfilment of our 'natures'; etc. The value of an action or object is then seen as derivative: an act gains value so far as it yields the relevant return to the actor; an object gains value by yielding that return to the persons who experience it. The parallel with work (act) and wages (value) is suggestive.

Given an input orientation, it is important to identify the group of creatures capable of experiencing, realizing, or receiving value. In saying that current value theory is man-centred I mean that this group is largely identified with the group of humans. Some accept that there are creatures other than men who experience pleasure or satisfaction or to whom the category of self-realization applies, and that therefore they too – higher mammals, for example – receive value. But such acknowledgment is usually in the nature of a postscript or footnote not seriously incorporated into the theory.

Generally speaking, then, the present view is that in engaging in the business (or game) of evaluating, commending, condemning, recommending, and appraising actions, the appropriate procedure is to refer to the results of the actions for men, with the understanding that the relevant results are such as pleasure, or satisfaction in one or more of various senses, or human self-realization, etc.[1] Two large issues thus arise and locate much of the debate within current value theory. First, specifically *what* kind of results count? Is it pleasure alone that matters? Or preference? Or self-realization? Second, how are the relevant results to be amalgamated? Is an action made right simply by the quantity of good results it produces? Or does the distribution of those results through the class of significant recipients matter? And, if so, what kind of distribution is preferable? A perfectly even distribution? Ought good results to be proportioned to desert? And, if so, what is the appropriate measure of desert?

In the foregoing chapters I have frequently objected to both of these features of current value theory and have taken positions that are inconsistent with them. Against the assumption of the dominance of man I have held that species other than man count too, and this in two respects: (1) individuals of other species count in the same general way that human individuals do; and (2) species other than man count – qua species even if not qua individuals. Moreover, inanimate features of the natural world count as well: elements of wilderness areas such as rocks and lakes that are not alive but form the setting in which species we wish to preserve live. In saying that these 'count' I mean that the ways they are affected by our actions are relevant to the appraisal of those actions – relevant *finally*, and not just in view of further ramifications for men.

Against the assumption of the dominance of interest I have held that in a

1 In an influential paper, 'The Point of View of Morality,' *Australasian Journal of Philosophy*, XXXII (1954), Kurt Baier writes that 'one of the principles by which we test group moralities [is] that a genuine moral rule must be *for the good* of human beings' (p. 126). Baier regards this principle as a necessary condition in the sense that if a moral rule isn't 'for the good of human beings' then it isn't 'genuine.' And W.D. Falk, in 'Morality, Self, and Others,' in *Morality and the Language of Conduct*, ed. H. Castañeda and G. Nakhnikian (Detroit, 1963), insists 'that a morality, if by this we mean a reasoned body of action-guiding principles and commitments, is always a morality for someone; and a morality for humans is one for humans' (p. 52).

On the face of it, this is a dreadful howler, equivocating between 'morality for humans' in the sense of a morality that is *for human guidance*, and 'morality for humans' in the sense of a morality that exists for *the good of humans*. But since in the context Falk is contrasting focusing on 'one's own good' and on 'the good of others', it would be more charitable to say that he didn't intend the sentence as an argument but was merely groping for a clever manner of putting his point. Whether howler or *bon mot*, though, it implies what Baier asserts, that rules that direct us, finally, to worry about the condition of anything other than human beings are either not moral rules or bad moral rules. Anyone familiar with the literature could produce dozens of similar examples.

professionalized occupation a person aims not so much to please or satisfy an audience, client, or user, even if this be the entire race, as to create an admirable object or to perform in an admirable manner, in the sense of measuring up to or even exceeding criteria for success developed by the occupation or by the person himself in his practice. I have held, for example, that a cook, ideally, will not simply judge his success by the degree to which his cooking pleases the people in the dining room, even if these are the only ones in any way affected by his activity; rather, he will aim at a professional ideal and will regard people's pleasure as relevant mainly so far as, by being the reaction of qualified judges, it confirms that he has done well. In this case the pleasure is evidence of success; the success consists in the fact the dish was prepared well, not in the fact that it pleased. Thus, the input orientation is replaced by one that holds that value 'belongs' to the object or to the activity by which it was created - which we may call, for contrast, an output orientation. And this same output orientation is met in the interpretation given to the ideas of responsibility and leisure.

Among the questions that need to be explored, then, are the following: Why should creatures other than man, as individuals and as species, and even inanimate things, 'count'? And if the input orientation is given up, if occupations are not to be judged by their results-for-man, what criteria for successful, not to say admirable, performance are available as reasonable alternatives? (What otherwise would show that objects or ways of acting - such as soufflés or 'performance in the surgery' - are admirable?) These are very large questions and obviously I can't hope to settle them definitively here. But it is necessary to indicate how they might be answered and to suggest a plausible line of reasoning in support of the answers.

II

The beginning of wisdom in these matters consists in recognition that the assumptions of the dominance of interest and of man are quite problematic. We can't sensibly begin our investigation by supposing that there is a prima facie case for the view that an action is right so far as it yields beneficial results for men, but not for any alternative view. 'Why does man count?' is fully as relevant to ask as is 'Why do things other than man count?'[2] Similarly, 'Why does

2 My thinking on this matter was opened up by the interesting discussion by Robert Nozick in *Anarchy, State, and Utopia* (New York, 1974), chap. 3. The notion of 'one life to live,' to which I refer, is developed in an appealing way by Michael Tooley, 'Abortion and Infanticide,' *Philosophy & Public Affairs*, II, no 1 (Fall 1972), pp. 37-65. Tooley sees this condition as grounded in a conception of self, and holds, roughly, that creatures (infants, for example) that have no conception of self have no serious right to live.

pleasure count?' is fully as relevant to ask as is 'What shows that (some) soufflés are admirable independently of their results-for-men?' For the most part, the assumptions of the dominance of interest and of man are uncriticized presuppositions, not reasoned conclusions.

Indeed, if we think in terms of prima facie cases, we are likely to conclude that the positions taken here, in opposition to the assumptions of the dominance of interest and of man, are the only initially plausible ones to hold. For if we forget about current value theory and look instead at the ways people actually use value language in their everyday lives, and at their actual practice of evaluating their activity and that of others, then we will find little evidence for the opinion that only results-for-men are *regarded* as important. Conscientious cooks do take the view ascribed to them, as do performers in the arts, scientists, and persons in numerous other occupations, including philosophers of value. On this concrete level, in reflections by people about what shows or would show that their own lives are admirable, almost no one is inclined to let the whole matter rest on the kind, quantity, and distribution of results-for-men their lives are responsible for. This means both that the prevalent attitude is that things other than men *do* count for something and that actions and objects have value owing to their satisfying perhaps dimly comprehended criteria, but nevertheless criteria that emphatically don't exclusively refer to *results-for-men*.

Against the background of these facts about our value-practice, it seems reasonable to hold that the problem isn't so much one of *demonstrating* the falsity of the assumptions of the dominance of interest and of man as it is of making comprehensible the fact that our practice is inconsistent with them. What we want is an *account* of our practice. Thus, if there exists an identifiable class of objects whose fate we regard as relevant to the evaluation of our actions, then we want to know, for example, what characteristics are common and peculiar to them all and are in addition such that were any of them to lose any of those characteristics we would no longer regard their fate as relevant. Such an account would at least form a good start toward developing a plausible alternative theory of value.

1 Bentham held that all sentient creatures count, and that what counts are their experiences of pleasure and pain – our actions are right so far as they bring pleasure to whatever is capable of experiencing it, wrong so far as they bring pain. But a more fundamental question should be put. Why do pain and pleasure count? And why do they *alone* count? If we could imagine someone utterly indifferent to pain – as the Stoics aspired to be – indifferent not merely in that he suffers it willingly in order to enjoy some benefit the suffering brings, but in that he doesn't *suffer* it at all, then we would not imagine that

his pain counts. (No doubt many would want to add that for him it isn't *pain*.) Similarly, if we could imagine someone utterly indifferent to pleasure – as Antisthenes aspired to be – in the same sense that pleasure as such simply doesn't matter to him, then we would not imagine that his pleasures count. The pains and pleasures people experience are regarded by us as relevant, as counting, because we sense that those pains and pleasures matter to them, that they *care* whether they have them.

If we take Bentham as our point of departure, then, it would seem that we should hold that *individuals*, whether human or other, count if anything is capable of *mattering* to them, if they are capable of *caring about* anything. By showing that it cares, any creature morally individuates itself in our eyes. 'Caring about' is not merely behavioural but involves consciousness as well. Thus, the struggles of a lobster dropped into boiling water don't convince us it cares about its fate unless we suppose as well that it experiences the condition it is in. For it to care about its fate it must have some foreboding of it, and its struggle must be an attempt to forestall it. For it to care about its pain it must feel it and its struggle must be an attempt to relieve it. Thus there seem to be two elements: consciousness and effort or disposition to gain, retain, or avoid. Creatures capable of caring count, and what counts is whatever they do or may care about. Such creatures are morally relevant qua individuals.

The natural way to extend this suggestion would be to say that some creatures count for more than others on particular occasions because more of what they care about more deeply is at stake. And prima facie some creatures (humans) count for considerably more than others because by having a conception of the conditions on which their lives as a whole would be meaningful many of the things that happen to them matter more profoundly than do things that happen to creatures without such a conception. The lobster's pain is for it at most a transient episode: the pain is not sensed as implicating a future that matters – and hence can't be imagined to matter as much – because it doesn't know a future, doesn't conceive itself as having 'one life to live.' A great deal turns on whether a creature remembers a past and contemplates a future through which it imagines that it will remain itself.

But if it is not the pain but the caring about the pain that is relevant (its painfulness, as some would say), and similarly for pleasure, then there is no basis for assigning an ultimate status to pain and pleasure in value theory. For plenty of other things matter as well: we might find ourselves *caring* about anything whatever.

In some such fashion as this we may mark out an approximate class of creatures that count qua individuals. However the position is developed in detail we may expect that others than humans will belong to the class, but that within the class humans will, in general, count for more, generally considerably more, than the other members of it.

2 But I have also held that species other than man count, as do certain inanimate things. Here they count not as individuals but as species, or things of a kind, and what is at stake is simply preservation of the species or of the kind. Why is this important? Why, *apart from human use*, is it important to preserve wilderness areas and species threatened by extinction? Certainly few think that all threatened species and all wilderness areas should be preserved. *Some* insects we are well rid of. And if a few examples of some kind of wilderness area are preserved and we are confident they can be held in their natural state, then the case for holding more, so far as it is based on grounds other than those that appeal to human use, is quite weak. (To be more accurate we should refer here not to 'human' use but to use by or on behalf of 'creatures that count qua individuals.')

When human use is ignored, three distinct lines of argument remain. First, there is a museum interest: it is something like making a collection. Preserving a species involves making sure that there will always be samples of that kind. The same holds true of seeking to preserve at least one of each kind of wilderness area. Second, there is an aesthetic motive: we regard some natural areas and some species as beautiful and wish to preserve them for the same reason we wish to preserve a beautiful thing that is man-made.

But third, and most significantly, an interest in preserving other species and certain inanimate things expresses an attitude toward 'not-man' that is inevitable if we adopt a non-exploitative stance – that is, if we reject the view that places humans on one side of a line and everything else on the other side, and then identifies the humans as persons, creatures who are ends in themselves, and identifies the rest as mere utilities that exist solely to serve human ends. What reasons have we for rejecting this view and adopting the non-exploitative stance? Five will be mentioned.

1 The stance is consonant with our considered judgments regarding the appropriate way of relating with 'not-man.' Since Sidgwick, perhaps since Kant, it has increasingly been accepted in ethical theory that people's considered judgments regarding concrete moral problems are data for ethical theorizing. This is not to say that any incongruity between what we conscientiously believe about a specific moral issue and some ethical theory invalidates the theory – but it does count against it. And a theory's success in accounting for most of our considered judgments (in some views, the 'deliverances of our moral sense') is a strong mark in its favour. Without this assumption of the (qualified) relevance of our considered judgments, there might still be some rational basis for reasoning about moral matters, but there would be no *data*, and the result for theory would be scepticism; just as, if one accepts Descartes' initial, corrosive universal doubt (by supposing that there may be a devil who is deliberately de-

ceiving him regarding every belief he holds) then all data disappear and in this vacuum there remains no purchase for fixing a tenable belief.

But among our considered judgments are numerous ones that involve our assigning value to conditions which, if we thought only in terms of human utility, we would have no good reason for preferring. It isn't aesthetics that makes us anxious about the survival of gorillas and baboons, and the museum argument is after all not very strong. But we have no reason to think the human race is better off with such creatures in the world than without them – in fact we know something of the utility, for Africans, of their extinction. None the less, we prefer their survival. And we extend this same view to the inanimate elements of wilderness areas and other natural environments.

2 The stance is the one suggested by reflection on the three broad problems considered in Chapters 2, 3, and 4. There I noted significant ambivalence between two typical but opposed attitudes in response to each of the problems: Shall we humanize technology or retreat back to nature? Shall we restore spatially defined community or endorse individualized lifestyles? Shall we humanize work or move toward a leisure-oriented society? In each case both alternatives are attractive. The advantage of the non-exploitative stance is that it gathers up the underlying features that we value in each of these alternatives, and in such a way that we are left with one coherent point of view toward all three of the problems.

3 As indicated earlier, the stance represents a fleshed-out form of objectivity – an actual manner of existing in the world that exemplifies the formal ideal of being objective, unbiased, impartial. The importance of this stems from the fact that there is a special connection between being objective and doing as we ought to do; namely, by definition, what a genuinely objective person prefers in some circumstances is what any one 'ought to' prefer in those circumstances. This conclusion is suggested by looking closely at what it is we are in doubt about when we question what we ought to do in any particular circumstances.

4 The non-exploitative stance is the appropriate one to take if we wish to live in a way that reflects the continuity of each man with the species man, with other species of living things, and with nature at large. By continuity here I mean simply a consequence of physical and biological facts, that all living things as it were come from one seed, that we literally carry that heritage around with us as a set of basic components of our own individual natures, and that life itself is nurtured in and emerges out of a highly special collection of physical conditions peculiar to this rather localized domain, Earth. Earth is a womb, and we are actualizations of potentialities it possessed for billions of

years before any life appeared on it. In adopting an exploitative stance vis-à-vis nature we act in a way that is simply insensitive to the continuity these facts suggest.

5 Finally, I think the non-exploitative stance is the defining trait of the ideal self any conscientious person will conceive when he emotionally incorporates the fact that his society has moved into an era of potential affluence constrained only by the finite character of our natural resources and of the capacity of Earth to absorb waste products. It is, however, neither a likely nor an appropriate stance for persons at an earlier stage of economic development to take. It is, one may say, the real luxury made possible by the astonishing productivity achieved in the West over the past few centuries.

III

A striking advantage of the assumptions of the dominance of interest and of man is that they give a generally clear-cut procedure for evaluating practices, including occupations. Indeed, this feature of utilitarianism is what primarily recommended it to Bentham. Virtually the only defence of the general utilitarian approach to practical decision-making that he could muster was the detailed argument, contained in a long footnote in Chapter 2 of *An Introduction to the Principles of Morals and Legislation*, to the effect that the major alternatives to utilitarianism are subjective in the sense that, lacking such a clear-cut procedure, they effectively reduce the making of moral judgments to the exercise of voicing private prejudices.[3]

How is the subjectivism Bentham feared to be avoided if we reject the enterprise of evaluating practices – in particular, occupations – by referring to their beneficial effects for some designated reference class, whether that class be coextensive with the class of men or broadened to include certain other animals – that is, if we replace the 'input orientation' by the view that people in their occupations are to concentrate not simply on 'results for people' but also on 'production of admirable objects'?

One possible answer, that suggested by the idea of 'objectivism,' must be ruled out. Some hold that 'good' is a simple quality or property that some things, actions, and conditions objectively *have*, in the same rough way that they have size and mass. Then the epistemological problem of explaining our knowledge that things have the quality is dealt with by positing a special, moral sense by or through which we discern that quality in the things, actions, and conditions that have it. Objectivism would make it possible to hold that prac-

3 *The Works of Jeremy Bentham* (Edinburgh, 1843), I, pp. 8-10.

tices, including occupations, get their value from the fact that the activities they involve and the objects they produce possess the objective quality good, rather than from their desirable effects in any other sense. Then, for example, one might claim that the cook I have referred to, who aims to dish up good food in some sense that doesn't reduce simply to the attempt to please his clients by means of the food, is in fact trying to prepare food that has the objective quality good.

I shall simply state without elaboration my reason for ruling out this solution. If objectivism is to provide an adequate account of our moral judgments it must suggest a means of distinguishing between two kinds of cases: those where one prefers some condition but it lacks the objective quality good, and those where one prefers the condition and it possesses that quality. The problem is that of how anyone, including the individual with the preference, is able to decide, when confronted with a preference, which of the two cases is before him – a preference with the objective quality, or a preference without it. How, that is, are we to decide of anything whatever of which we approve, whether it also has the objective quality good? There seems to be no criterion to appeal to here, and a natural conclusion to draw is that the supposed objective quality simply doesn't exist. In the absence of such a criterion, it would be gratuitous to interpose the objective quality between our preferences and the perceived qualities that in any case account for them.

But is there a third alternative, besides objectivism and the subjectivist view that the so-called 'admirableness' of soufflés and surgical performances consists simply in the fact that the person who makes the claim admires or likes them?

Here again a useful corrective to the tenor of much philosophical discussion of this matter – as conducted by amateur and professional philosophers alike – consists in looking to the facts of people's lives in their occupations. Certainly people seldom take the view of their own occupation that any way of carrying it on is equally as good, correct, or admirable as any other. What one often notices instead is a strong sense of standards for success and for admirable performance. Notions about how cooking, doing scientific research, lecturing, sweeping floors, conducting trials and arguing legal cases, defending philosophical beliefs, painting pictures, painting walls, cataloguing books, firing furnaces, selling second-hand cars, editing manuscripts, or fighting fires *ought to be done* are not regarded by the people who do them as wholly arbitrary or conventional, or as gaining their whole sense from the good-results-for-men they produce.

In some occupations, social service, for example, there is a primary commitment to 'human benefit.' But a scientist could make little sense of his working day if he had to link everything he does ultimately to the good-for-man he does. His primary commitment, rather, is to something like 'truth.' Similarly, a musician hopes people will enjoy his music, but his primary commitment, we may say, for want of a more specific term, is 'beauty.' The traditional categories by which the entire field of values is classified – the good, the true, and the beautiful – don't cover all the cases, however. None has a natural application to the primary commitments of the cook, the editor, or the janitor. And yet who is to say that the values possessed by competent performance of these occupations and by their results aren't fully as *serious* as those we associate with scientific theories and recitals?

A normative theory that more closely approximates the *structure* of our lives than utilitarianism does would need to be based on a fundamental distinction between two sorts of 'rules' that bear on the conduct of occupations: performance rules and side constraints.[4] The former incorporate the method of the occupation, the 'state-of-the-art.' It is this that, for example, the student of one of the special sciences primarily learns: how best to *do* the science.

By developing a conception of its own method and goals, an occupation creates as it were a world and a logic of its own. These are not fixed, once and for all, but are subject to constant revision, and the logic of the occupation serves also to make sense of or condemn revisions proposed. This is not to say that every move and every development are rigidly prescribed. Not everything can be, needs to be, or should be justified. Sports, spontaneity, arbitrariness are tolerable in every occupation, and some feed on it. But when an occupation acquires a method that its practitioners share, one relevant to its own proper concerns and not to extrinsic goals, then it gains the common ground on which to settle specific questions about competent, efficient, successful, admirable performance and results. By acquiring such a method it makes it the case that not everything done in the occupation is arbitrary. It is only outsiders, unaware of the method and insensitive to the logic of the process by which it reached its present state and by which it will undergo further development, who mistakenly characterize what goes on inside as conventional, arbitrary, and subjective. Philosophers of science, whose business it is to comprehend this 'logic' as developed in the sciences, and art historians and critics, similarly concerned with the 'logic' of creativity in the arts, don't make this mistake.[5]

4 The term 'side constraints' is suggested by Nozick, *Anarchy, State, and Utopia*, p. 29. There is a formal similarity between the two kinds of rules discussed here and his contrast between side constraints and moral goals. But the differences far outweigh the similarities.

5 Thomas Kuhn, *The Structure of Scientific Revolutions* (2nd ed., Chicago, 1970), and others have argued that at critical points in the history of a science paradigm shifts occur that revolutionize the science, and that this process is not defensible in the normal way – in a sense, not defensible at all. The implication is that even science, in the last analy-

But numerous other occupations have also achieved a generally understood method that similarly grounds a distinction between success and failure, the excellent and the mediocre, the admirable and the trite, in their own spheres.

Side constraints are just that, constraints placed on the method to assure that the side effects of practising it are acceptable. For the most part, side constraints are *moral* rules, and it is in this connection that 'results-for-man,' the assumptions of the dominance of interest and of man (and other mammals), are relevant. Performance rules (the method) have very little to do with morals but rather express an historically developed view of how the occupation is best carried on in the interest of achieving the goals it conceives, goals the specific definition of which are also historically developed and in process of reformulation. Not every occupation has a method that bears on its own proper goals rather than such extrinsic purposes as those of making money or glorifying the nation. But adequately professionalized occupations have. And any occupation capable of professionalization is also capable of achieving such a method.

For the individual, development by the occupation of a method, performance rules, means that he gains a *craft*. He may then orient himself toward his craft: toward doing it properly, excellently; toward reaching the craft-goals, exceeding them; toward improving the craft and refining its goals, so that he leaves it in a better state than it was in when he picked it up. These concerns focus his life and in them he finds his true 'morality.'[6] The side constraints, by

sis, is 'subjective': its pronouncements are relative to a paradigm the acceptability of which is not capable of being established by 'scientific methods.' But Stephen Toulmin, *Human Understanding* (Oxford, 1972), I, has argued persuasively that this view rests on an absolutistic conception of 'rationality.' His alternative, which restores the qualified rationality of science, involves taking seriously the respects in which science is a *social institution* (an occupation). It appears that the line of argument he develops must apply as well to occupations other than science, and apparently he intends in subsequent volumes to make this application. One may expect to find there a detailed working out of the view suggested here.

6 'A certain professor once said: "For me to be moral is to behave like a professor".' Strawson, 'Social Morality and Individual Ideal,' in *Philosophy*, XXXVI (1961), p. 8. Strawson's juxtaposition of 'social morality' and 'individual ideal' is fundamentally sympathetic to the present contrast between side constraints and performance rules. The differences largely result from his interest, in the article referred to, in capturing an important feature of libertarian society, the room in it for numerous conflicting images of an ideal life, no one of which is supposed to have any final advantage over any of the others. 'Social morality' then exists primarily to preserve this variety, to make it viable. My interest, by contrast, is to exhibit the *social* aspect of Strawson's 'individual ideal,' the way in which people's lives coalesce around such ideal images and the way in which the images become objectified in practices.

The apparent contradiction between associating morality with side constraints and also with 'performance rules' or objectivity is merely verbal. As Strawson's quotation contrast, aren't typically goals at all and may seldom come into view. For a person who has a craft and a profession the 'moral life,' as this is conventionally understood, is a minor theme: it doesn't catch up his primary goals, values, and concerns. When it does preoccupy him – when the need to notice and adapt to side constraints becomes insistent – then new commitments enter that may well dominate professional commitments. But these are none the less basically distractions from the main 'business' at hand, the craft.[7] In the best of circumstances, morals are just a nuisance.

makes clear, 'morality' just happens to be used in two very different ways. There is a deeper issue, however. A traditional view holds that the 'good man' is, above all, a *moral* man in the first-mentioned sense, one who adheres scrupulously to all the relevant side constraints. This view is sometimes contrasted with a classical Greek conception – especially associated with Aristotle's catalogue of the moral virtues and their accompanying vices – which identifies the good man as one who has developed in his own character those habits that determine anyone to be distinctively human. Thus, the good man is courageous rather than a coward or foolhardy, manifests proper pride rather than undue humility, practise magnificence rather than vulgar display or niggardliness, and, of course, thinks a lot, especially in a philosophical vein. The main difference between the two views is that the first makes being a good man turn on what you do for or to others, or on what you intend to do. The second makes being a good man turn on *what* what you do discloses about yourself, whether, in a now outmoded sense, it shows you to be *manly*. Both views, however, treat how you conduct yourself in your occupation, your conduct as an employee, craftsman, or professional, as generally irrelevant to your qualifications as a good man.

By contrast, my view is that being professional in one's occupation is a central condition of being a good man. In the fullest sense, the good man is the objective man. His objectivity is shown in his leisureliness, in his stance of responsibility vis-à-vis nature, and above all through his professional conduct in his occupation. It is understood of course that the occupation is not socially undesirable or otherwise reprehensible, and that the person's activity in all three connections is sensitive to the relevant side constraints. My position is therefore closer to the classical Greek one than to the other, in our tradition, Christian conception of a good man. The primary exception to the claim made above, that Aristotle regarded one's occupational activity as generally irrelevant to one's qualifications as a good man, is the case where one's occupation is that of a philosopher. Consequently, the recommended view largely results from dropping the notion that man has a nature which dictates that he can become fully himself only in a contemplative life, and replacing that with the assumption that our 'nature' is sufficiently open to permit our becoming ourself in a virtually endless number of diverse occupations. But then it isn't the fact that by taking it up we will 'become ourself' that recommends the occupation to us.

7 In the interest of making a point I am overstating it. Occupations generally aren't as unrelated to their surroundings as these remarks suggest. A very important respect in which this is true is that social needs, the meeting of which is required by a profession's side constraints, are often defined by the profession. Thus, a service and benefit to the community that courts of law provide is procedural justice. But the meaning of procedural justice is given by the 'method' that in the course of time our legal practices have evolved. Similarly, the need for good food that the cooking 'craft' meets is to a degree defined by that craft. Obviously, this point shouldn't be pushed too far: we aren't necessarily healthy because the doctor says we are.

Index